abc

7th Edition

Air Band
Radio Guide

D1464592

Graham Duke

MIDLAND

An imprint of
Ian Allan Publishing

Contents

First published 1992
7th edition first published 2009

ISBN 978 1 85780 319 8

All rights reserved. No part of this book may be reproduced or transmitted in any form or by any means, electronic or mechanical, including photocopying, recording or by any information storage and retrieval system, without permission from the Publisher in writing.

© Graham Duke 2009

Published by Midland Publishing

an imprint of Ian Allan Publishing Ltd,
Hersham, Surrey KT12 4RG.
Printed by Ian Allan Printing Ltd,
Hersham, Surrey KT12 4RG.

Code: 0910/B3

Visit the Ian Allan Publishing website at:
www.ianallanpublishing.com

1. The UK Airspace System

Before examining the subject of airband radio and other monitoring systems, an overview of the processes involved in handling air traffic may help to give a better understanding of how it all works. Most *en route* traffic operating in UK airspace, including the surrounding sea areas, is managed from Air Traffic Control centres at Swanwick (Hampshire), Prestwick (Ayrshire), and Manchester International Airport. Traffic in the Republic of Ireland is the responsibility of a centre at Shannon (Southern Ireland).

General Aviation flights, including light aircraft, helicopters, gliders and balloons, are usually dealt with at local level, from air traffic controllers at airports, and Flight Information Service Officers or radio operators at the smaller airfields. The UK and Northern Ireland is divided into two control areas, *London*, managed from Swanwick, and *Scottish*, managed from Prestwick. Each region is known as a Flight Information Region or FIR. These are split at flight level 245 (FL245 - approximately 24,500 feet) into lower and upper airspace. The upper airspace is referred to as Upper Flight Information Regions or UIRs, although the term FIR is generally used to describe both upper and lower airspace.

The London FIR includes England and Wales to 55 degrees North, approximately in line with Newcastle-upon-Tyne. North of this line is the Scottish FIR, which also covers a large area of the sea to the north of Scotland, and is in fact the largest control area in Europe. Both FIRs extend to the boundaries of the adjacent European FIRs to the south and east of the British Isles. The Manchester centre lies within the London FIR, having responsibility for traffic in an extensive portion of central England up to FL 285.

To the west of the British Isles, the eastern half of the North Atlantic is the responsibility of the Shanwick Area Control Centre at Prestwick, using the callsign *'Shanwick'*.

London Stanstead Visual Control Room with Electronic Flight Strip displays
Courtesy of National Air Traffic Services

An Overview

UK airspace is subdivided into several categories, operating with various levels of service and a corresponding variety of radio messages. In many cases the words and phrases reflect the nature of the type of airspace in which they are used. Service categories range from the most basic, where pilots are given minimal information to assist them with their flight, through to the highest level where ATC assumes full responsibility for the safe separation of aircraft under its control.

There are seven international categories of airspace, lettered from A through to G. Class A airspace is subject to the highest level of control, and includes airways in lower airspace and terminal areas. In upper airspace, above flight level 245, the airspace is Class C, and aircraft are always provided with a full control service. There is no Class B airspace in the UK.

The remaining Classes D, E and F are subject to some kind of control, but Class G is not. Class G, which is sometimes referred to as 'free' airspace or the 'open' FIR, is all the lower airspace which is not covered by any of the other categories. Controllers and pilots never mention these different types of airspace but simply use the terms 'controlled' or 'uncontrolled' airspace.

The various elements of service to pilots are as follows:

The Visual Control Room, Edinburgh airport
Courtesy of National Air Traffic Services

Flight Information Services

There are four levels of service to pilots operating outside controlled airspace:

- Basic
- Traffic
- Deconfliction
- Procedural

The simplest is the Basic Service, where pilots are only given information about the weather and so on. A Traffic Service is the Basic Service, plus information on other known flights. At the next level, under a Deconfliction Service, pilots are given advice on avoiding other aircraft. Finally, under a Procedural Service, flights in Class F airspace, which are in contact with ATC, are separated from each other based on position reports from pilots.

TRY SOMETHING DIFFERENT

Scanning?
Listening?
Try Transmitting?

Many think of becoming an amateur radio operator as something hard to achieve but this just isn't the case. Amateur radio in the UK has never been more accessible and you could easily be on the air talking to the world right now. All UK licences provide access to a wide range of radio bands including HF for worldwide communications, in fact through the spectrum from microwaves to LF.

Amateur radio is endlessly fascinating and getting "on the air" opens a whole new world to you, enabling you to make friends all over the world, build your own equipment, install your own amateur radio station and participate in the hobby in whatever way you want. You could try:

✔ Emergency Communications
✔ Amateur Radio Satellites
✔ International Space Station
✔ Data Communication
✔ Direction Finding
✔ Contests
✔ Awards
✔ And much, much, more!

All that is needed is a pass at Foundation level to access amateur radio and this can be achieved in as little as a weekend. The Foundation level even provides training in basic operating that gets you "on the air", so you know how to operate when you get a licence. All that is required beyond the practical elements provided in the training is that you pass a straightforward test of 25 multiple choice questions. There is nothing to be frightened of in the exam either, as we have had thousands pass in recent years, with some as young as 7 going on to be licensed radio amateurs.

There is nothing to stop you expanding your horizons so why not get into amateur radio?

For more information visit **www.rsgb.org/getlicence** or ring 01234 832 700 to be sent details of training and exams in your area.

This article was brought to you by the Radio Society of Great Britain
3 Abbey Court, Fraser Road, Priory Business Park, Bedford, MK44 3WH
Tel: 01234 832 700

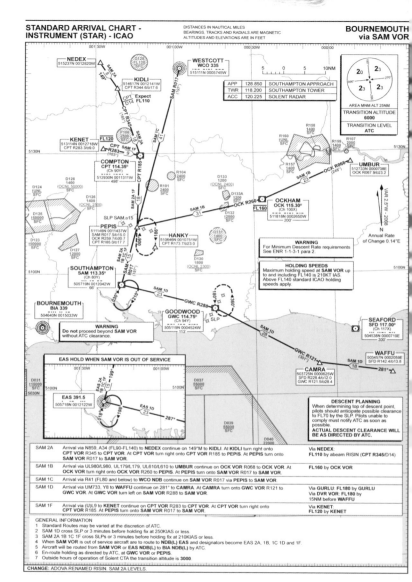

Chart for the Bournemouth Standard
Arrival Route via Southampton
Courtesy of National Air Traffic Services

The Basic Service may be provided by air traffic control officers, flight information service officers and air/ground radio operators. The others may only be given by ATCOs, usually operating from local airports and airfields, and generally applies to low-level general aviation flights routing across the country, mostly in good visual conditions, complemented by a non-radar service given by the air traffic control centres in London and Scotland. These are known respectively as London Information and Scottish Information.

Radar may be used when providing a Basic Service, but it will be used for a Traffic or Deconfliction Service. A Procedural Service is a non-radar service. Flight Information Service Officers and Air/Ground radio operators operate from small local strips where there is no ATC service. An important principle for all these services is that where aircraft are operating in class F and class G airspace, it is not mandatory for an air traffic service to be provided; therefore pilots are solely responsible for collision avoidance and terrain clearance at all times.

Controlled Airspace

This term refers to any airspace where the air traffic controllers have some degree of responsibility for ensuring that aircraft remain separated from each other by

Birmingham Approach Control
Courtesy of National Air Traffic Services

10cm Radar, Birmingham
Courtesy of National Air Traffic Services

Manchester Visual Control Room
Courtesy of National Air Traffic Services

minimum standards. The level of their responsibility varies according to the airspace class, increasing to its maximum in Class A airspace where the controller provides a full service to every flight. Pilots are only permitted to fly in such airspace if they are qualified to fly on aircraft instruments, rather than visually, and the aircraft must be carrying certain types of navigation and surveillance equipment. Pilots must comply with instructions given by controllers regarding headings, changes of level and speed.

In Classes D and E airspace, certain rules still apply but they are less stringent than for Class A, allowing visual traffic, whose pilots may not be qualified to fly using instruments alone, to mix with passenger-carrying jet aircraft. For this reason, these types of airspace are sometimes referred to as Regulated Airspace. The airways system is a series of Class A airspace corridors, each at least ten nautical miles wide, extending from a variable base level up to flight level 195 (approximately 19,500ft). Above FL195, the airspace changes to Class C, in accordance with European standards, although the division between upper and lower airspace remains at FL245.

The variable base levels are designed to provide protection to traffic in the airways while at the same time allowing flights in Class G airspace to fly underneath them. The airway centre lines follow straight lines between radio navigation beacons or geographical positions, and they link major airports and provide cross-country routes both for domestic and international air traffic. Other controlled airspace exists around airports, with Terminal airspace where several airports are close together.

Upper Airspace

Above FL245 (approximately 24,500ft) the whole of the airspace is Class C and aircraft are provided with a full air traffic control service. The routes through this airspace generally follow the airways system below but many additional ones have been introduced to cater for the increasing number of flights and to provide more economical direct tracks. The upper airspace routes have no set dimensions, although they are deemed to be ten nautical miles wide.

The best shortwave radio magazine in the uk is crammed with airband columns and features every month!

■ www.radiouser.co.uk

radiouser

Combining the very best of both Short Wave Magazine & Radio Active

With all the best features, articles, news and reviews from two superb magazines together in one place, **radiouser** is not only a terrific read but also marvellous value for money.

IT'S OFFICIAL!
radiouser
is the best selling
radio listening
magazine in the UK!

Filled to the brim with radio, radio and more radio! Contents include:

- The SBS-1 Files
- Military Matters
- Sky High
- Airband News
- Reviews
- Features
- Scanning in Action
- Radio Questions & Answers

- Scanning Scene
- New Products
- News
- LM&S Broadcast Matters
- Websites
- Maritime Matters
- Info in Orbit
- Decode

- Comms From Europe
- Off the Record
- Software Spot
- DXTV
- NDB DXing
- Beginner's Guides
- Feedback
- Bookstore
- Trading Post

Practical Wireless is Britain's best selling amateur radio magazine

Contents include; Amateur Radio News, Products and Rally Information. The magazine also brings you regular reports on all the bands, antennas, historical, technical and feature articles and a comprehensive, fast Book Service.

Save Money! Joint subscriptions are now available

Available from UK newsagents, by subscription or direct from us

TEL: 0845 803 1979   FAX: 01202 659950   E-MAIL: info@pwpublishing.ltd.uk

Quality, value-for-money hobby radio magazines from PW Publishing Ltd.
PW Publishing Ltd., Arrowsmith Court, Station Approach, Broadstone, Dorset BH18 8PW, UK
web: www.pwpublishing.ltd.uk

North Atlantic Airspace

A different control system exists for traffic in oceanic airspace. Flights are controlled procedurally, meaning that controllers act on position reports from pilots at pre-set intervals. This is because radar operates on a line-of-sight principle; therefore aircraft are soon beyond the range of land-based radar stations. In order to take advantage of the North Atlantic weather conditions a series of eastbound and westbound routes, known as 'tracks', are set up every 24 hours, providing the most efficient and economical flight paths across the ocean.

The eastbound tracks are in place overnight, while the westbound tracks operate during the day. They can vary considerably from day to day, sometimes being to the north of the area, sometimes to the south, resulting in flights crossing the UK on different routes on consecutive days. Position reports are provided at set intervals, using either High Frequency radio or Controller-Pilot Datalink Communications or CPDLC. High Frequency (HF) radio has been in use for several decades since VHF radio depends on line of sight and therefore cannot be used.

However, HF is notoriously unpredictable and the quality can change from reasonably good to extremely poor in a relatively short

***The Iconic Tower
at Farnborough***
Courtesy of National Air Traffic Services

***VLM Fokker 50 on final
approach to London City***
Courtesy of National Air Traffic Services

period. Datalink messages, via VHF receivers or satellite technology, are more reliable and less prone to failures. HF datalink is particularly useful in regions where other systems are ineffective – over the polar regions, for example. HF transmissions between Shanwick and aircraft in the North Atlantic are routed via a radio station at Ballygirreen, near Shannon, originally set up to deal with the flying boats which landed in the Shannon estuary after crossing the Atlantic. Messages are relayed through radio officers at Ballygirreen, and controllers at Shanwick do not communicate directly with pilots when using HF. The callsign 'Shanwick' is a combination of the two locations, Shannon and Prestwick.

Position reports are made at each whole degree of longitude as the flight crosses the ocean, and this report is compared with the flight plan to ensure that there is no variation which could compromise the safety of other aircraft on the same track and at the same flight level. This process is now fully automatic, using sophisticated software at the oceanic control centres to monitor the traffic and issue alerts to controllers if potential problems seem to be developing. As well as the centre at Prestwick, other areas of the North Atlantic are handled by

Runway Visual Range Equipment, London City
Courtesy of National Air Traffic Services

centres at Gander, Santa Maria, New York and Iceland. Details of HF frequencies can be found in the appendices.

Cat 111 B Instrument Landing System at London Gatwick
Courtesy of National Air Traffic Services

Communications

The complexity of the air traffic system requires the use of a wide range of radio frequencies to handle the different functions needed to provide a flexible and efficient service to the different categories of flight. Over the UK and Europe, communication between controllers and pilots is by VHF radio. Military flights also use UHF for most of their operations. As both these systems depend on line of sight they can usually be heard on an airband receiver reasonably well in most parts of the United Kingdom, since aircraft transmitting above 20,000 feet will have a radio range in excess of 150 miles.

However, messages from controllers are less reliable simply because the ground based transmitters may be hidden from the receiver by buildings, hills, and so on. In many parts of the country, receiving ATC transmissions is difficult or even impossible. Although there are a number of options for enhancing weak signals which can go a long way towards solving the problem, investing more money in the equipment often has no effect. These aspects are examined throughout the book.

Further Reading

If you are interested in learning more about the procedures and systems in use today you will probably find the companion publication *abc Air Traffic Control* helpful. It describes in considerably more detail the UK air traffic system and its management.

(This page)
**The Visual Control Room,
London Gatwick** Courtesy of National Air Traffic Services

2. The Legal Position

Introduction

The Office of Communications is the government body responsible for regulating all types of communications in the UK. It came into existence at the end of 2003, and took over the roles of five other regulators, one of which was the Radiocommunications Agency.

The primary piece of legislation covering the use of receive-only radio equipment is the Wireless Telegraphy Act 2006. There is considerable misunderstanding among the general public regarding the ownership and use of airband scanners, so the following questions and answers may be helpful:

Any apparatus designed for the receipt of aviation messages is considered to be an aeronautical station under the terms of the UK Air Navigation Order and as such requires the approval of the Civil Aviation Authority. The CAA, however, only recognise receiving stations that are required to provide an aeronautical service as being suitable for approval, therefore any other person or organisation will not be successful in applying for such authorisation.

The Air Navigation Order (ANO) and the Wireless Telegraphy Act 2006 both specifically prohibit the use of radio apparatus capable of receiving aeronautical messages.

Q. Am I breaking the law if I buy a scanner?

A. No, there is nothing illegal about owning a scanner.

Q. Can I listen to air traffic control messages?

A. No, you must only listen to public broadcasts such as the BBC.

Q. Is it OK if I do not disclose the information I hear?

A. No, the act of listening is itself illegal.

Q. Can I apply for a licence to use my airband scanner?

A. No, licences are not available to members of the public.

Q. Can the authorities confiscate my scanner?

A. Yes, but they would have to prove you were using it illegally. If the scanner also receives public broadcasts this would be difficult.

Q. Why are scanners readily available if using them is against the law?

A. Radio equipment is covered by EEC regulations which permit them to be sold.

Q. How many people have been prosecuted recently?

A. Accurate and reliable information is hard to come by, but few, if any, successful prosecutions have taken place in the last few years.

Q. Why aren't more people being prosecuted?

A. The authorities recognise that in most cases the use of a scanner is part of a harmless pastime. Aircraft operations are not affected and they do not cause interference to other radio users.

There are two criminal offences, under section 48 of the Wireless Telegraphy Act 2006, relating to unauthorised reception.

It is an offence if a person,
'otherwise than under the authority of a designated person
.... uses wireless telegraphy apparatus with intent to obtain information as to the contents, sender or addressee of any message whether sent by means of wireless telegraphy or not, of which neither the person using the apparatus nor a person on whose behalf he is acting is an intended recipient.'

It is also an offence for someone, otherwise than under the authority of a designated person, to disclose any information as to the contents, sender or addressee of any message referred to in the above paragraph. This means that it is also illegal to tell a third party what has been heard in a transmission a person has listened to illegally. There is a common misunderstanding that it is acceptable to listen to non-broadcast messages provided the information is not passed on to anyone else, but this is not the case. The act of listening is in itself an offence.

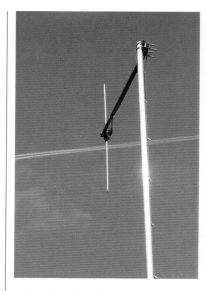

A simple but effective VHF antenna
Author

Libyan Airlines Canadair-CRJ-900 about to depart from Manchester Author

Going abroad?

The UK authorities seem to take a relaxed view on the use of airband scanners, recognising that they are part of a harmless hobby and that there is no intention of using the information derived from using the equipment for any suspicious purposes. However, foreign countries often have a much more serious view of airband listening and it is highly likely that it would be classed as an act of espionage in some places, especially near military establishments.

Conclusion

At the present time, the authorities appear not to take very much interest in people who choose to listen to air traffic control transmissions, but it has to be remembered that it is illegal and could lead to prosecution. Always be discreet if using a scanner and respect others who may be annoyed by the constant radio chatter. For more detailed information on the legal position, contact the Office of Communications (Ofcom) at the address given in the appendices, or visit www.ofcom.org.uk

Airbus aircraft of Turkish Airlines
Author

3. How the System Works

The Division of Airspace

All airspace across the UK and Europe is divided into Upper Airspace and Lower Airspace, separated at Flight Level 245 (FL245) approximately equal to 24,500 feet. The airspace of Scotland and Northern Ireland is the responsibility of a Control Centre at Prestwick, Scotland, using the callsign 'Scottish'. Airspace over England and Wales is the responsibility of a Control Centre at Swanwick, near Fareham in Hampshire, using the callsign 'London'. Part of the London area is delegated to a sub-centre at Manchester airport, with the callsign 'Manchester'. Individual airports and airfields have their own callsigns for the different functions – for example, Newcastle Airport has Newcastle Radar, Newcastle Approach, Newcastle Tower and so on.

In upper airspace (known as the Upper Flight Information Region, abbreviated to UIR) all traffic is under mandatory radar control of one of these centres. Flights in lower airspace (the Flight Information Region or FIR) operate under varying levels of control according to the type of flight and the class of airspace. Upper and lower airspace together are usually described as the FIR – for example, the 'London FIR'. Lower airspace is divided into several categories - for example, the airspace around airfields, airways, advisory routes, military training areas, danger areas and so on.

Traffic flying in the airways system is afforded the highest level of control, using radar surveillance, where controllers have a legal responsibility to ensure that aircraft are safely separarted from each other by minimum prescribed distances. Airways are often desribed as the motorways of the skies, providing protected routes across the UK and Europe. They are at least ten nautical

Unlike most other UK airports, Manchester actively encourages spectators at the Aviation Viewing Park Author

miles wide, with stepped base levels according to their location and purpose. The upper limit of the airways is FL245.

The airspace is also broken down into a number of geographical regions, known as sectors, where teams of controllers manage the traffic within each sector using a dedicated radio frequency. As aircraft cross the country, the responsibility for control is passed from one group of sector controllers to the next, with the appropriate change of radio frequency. A large proportion of UK airspace is also divided into vertical sectors, so that aircraft at different flight levels will be under the control of different sector teams. Airports have their own individual teams of controllers who handle traffic departing from, or arriving at, the airfield, or transiting the region at low levels.

Air Traffic Services

Most aircraft will be in radio contact with air traffic controllers, but in Class G airspace some pilots may not be communicating with anybody, as they are not obliged to do so. Although they are usually referred to by the general term 'controllers', in many cases ATC personnel do not have direct control over the aircraft with which they are in contact. This

Swiss BAE146 on finals to
Manchester runway 23 right
Author

depends on the class in which the aircraft is flying. In certain types of airspace the controller may be merely providing appropriate flight information or advice even though the airspace may be referred to as 'controlled'. Sometimes this airspace is described as 'regulated' instead of controlled.

Certain other persons are also permitted to talk to pilots by radio, such as Air/Ground Radio Operators and Aerodrome Flight Information Service Officers, but neither of these can give instructions to pilots. Messages between controllers and flightcrews vary in content according to the service being provided. Controllers' messages are transmitted from a number of stations located across the UK, and many of these are at civil and military airfields, where the personnel may provide a service to flights using the airfield or passing through the area. Some radio stations are located at remote sites across the country, often operating from the same sites as radar stations.

(Above) **China Airlines A330-243 (B-6093) in Star Alliance colours on finals for runway 27 left at London Heathrow**
Shaun Grist

(Below) **Aer Arran late arrival at Prestwick**
Courtesy of National Air Traffic Services

Radio Telephony Procedures

Over the years, radiotelephony has developed and evolved in response to a changing environment and through the experiences gained in investigating incidents and accidents where misunderstandings and errors in communication have been a factor.

As traffic levels rise, the emphasis on ensuring safe systems increases and language is a critical element in the equation. It is vitally important that communications between pilots and controllers are clear and unambiguous if the risk of compromising safety is to be minimised.

Carelessness with language and failure to follow correct operating procedures still account for a number of serious incidents every year. For this reason, many of the terms used in air traffic control have very specific meanings, some of which are detailed here. More detailed and comprehensive descriptions can be found in *abc Air Traffic Control*.

Word/phrase	Meaning
Level	A general term describing the vertical distance of an aircraft.
Flight Level	The approximate level at which an aircraft is flying, spoken with the last two digits omitted. For example, 32,000 feet is spoken as Flight Level 320. Flight levels apply to aircraft flying above the Transition Level, usually 3,000ft or 6,000ft in the UK.
Altitude	The vertical distance of an aircraft above mean sea level, when flying below the Transition Level.
Height	The vertical distance of an aircraft above the ground (usually the runway) when flying below the Transition Level.
QNH	Barometric air pressure in millibars, applied when flying at altitudes.
QFE	Barometric air pressure in millibars, applied when flying at heights.
Climb/Descend	Increase or decrease the level of an aircraft.
Maintain	Remain at the present level.
Heading	The direction, in degrees, on which an aircraft is flying.
Radar Heading	A specific heading instructed by air traffic control.
Continue	Continue at the present radar heading.
Mach number	The speed of an aircraft in terms of the speed of sound, which is equal to Mach 1. For example, Mach decimal 82 is 82 per cent of the speed of sound. The actual speed varies depending on level and temperature.
Monitor	Listen out on a specified radio frequency and wait for a controller to make contact.
Contact	Report to a controller on a specified radio frequency.
Squawk	A four-digit number entered by the pilot into a radio transponder to assist with radar identification.
Squawk Ident	Causes the aircraft data block on the radar screen to flash, assisting with identification.

Aer Arran aircraft taxying at Manchester Author

Aeronautical Radio Frequencies

There are 760 Very High Frequency (VHF) channels allocated for international civil aeronautical use, plus a number of other special channels which have been introduced across Europe in order to meet an increasing shortage. Because each frequency used for high-level traffic has a range in excess of 150 miles it is important that the same ones are not allocated within this distance; therefore there are simply not enough to meet present-day requirements in spite of careful planning at a European level.

Under the conventional system of 760 channels, the separation between each of them is 25kHz. To meet the shortage across Europe, in October 1999 additional channels were provided between the existing ones, with spacings of 8.33 kHz. This, of course, meant that every aircraft flying in European airspace had to be fitted with radios that could cope with both systems, and pilots had to understand that they used quite different methods of operation. Attempting to transmit a message on the wrong radio caused severe interference and for a time there were numerous operational problems.

When the 8.33 kHz system was first introduced, it was referred to by controllers as 'channels', to distinguish it from the conventional 'frequencies'. This distinction has now been dropped. Another problem with the 8.33kHz system is the very narrow spacing between each channel, only one third of the conventional method which uses 25kHz spacing. Under the original system it was possible to transmit on the same frequency from two or three different transmitters, giving a wide coverage, using 'offset' frequencies. However, this is not practical with 8.33kHz spacing, where only one transmitter can be used.

This has practical implications for airband listening, which is considered in more detail later. Radio transmitters for each control centre are strategically located at sites across the UK and Ireland, designed to provide the most efficient coverage to the traffic in the area. At airfields, the radio transmitters are only effective over a comparatively short range, whereas the *en route* transmitters are much more powerful.

Reception of controllers' messages from one of these transmitters depends on the line-of-sight principle necessary for VHF

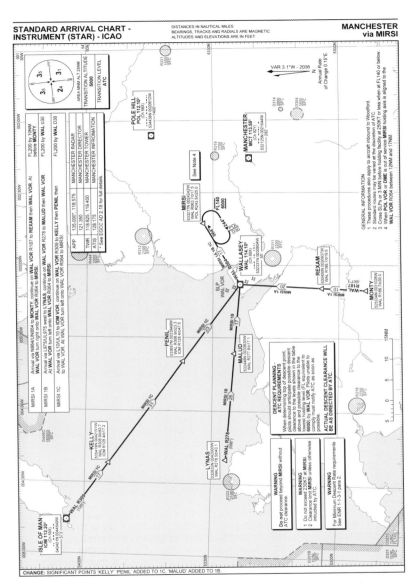

STANDARD ARRIVAL CHART - INSTRUMENT (STAR) - ICAO

DISTANCES IN NAUTICAL MILES
BEARINGS, TRACKS AND RADIALS ARE MAGNETIC
ALTITUDES AND ELEVATIONS ARE IN FEET

MANCHESTER via MIRSI

Standard Arrival Route chart via MERSI for Manchester
Courtesy of National Air Traffic Services

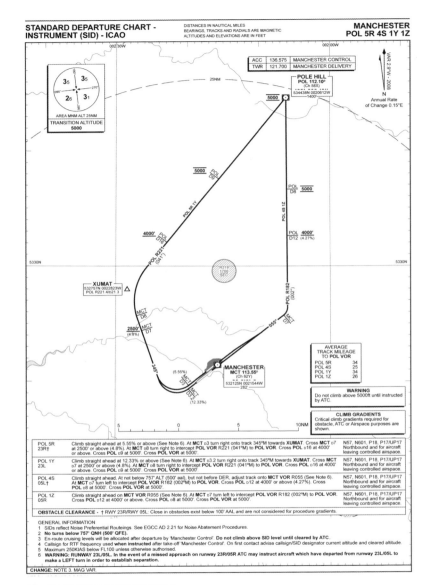

STANDARD DEPARTURE CHART - INSTRUMENT (SID) - ICAO

DISTANCES IN NAUTICAL MILES
BEARINGS, TRACKS AND RADIALS ARE MAGNETIC
ALTITUDES AND ELEVATIONS ARE IN FEET

MANCHESTER
POL 5R 4S 1Y 1Z

| ACC | 136.575 | MANCHESTER CONTROL |
| TWR | 121.700 | MANCHESTER DELIVERY |

AREA MNM ALT 25NM
TRANSITION ALTITUDE
5000

POLE HILL
POL 112.10°
(Ch 58X)
5344 38N 0020612W
14000'

VAR 2.9°W - 2008
N
Annual Rate
of Change 0.15°E

AVERAGE TRACK MILEAGE TO POL VOR

POL 5R	34
POL 4S	25
POL 1Y	34
POL 1Z	26

WARNING
Do not climb above 5000ft until instructed by ATC.

CLIMB GRADIENTS
Critical climb gradients required for obstacle, ATC or Airspace purposes are shown.

POL 5R 23R†	Climb straight ahead at 5.55% or above (See Note 6). At **MCT** D3 turn right onto track 345°M towards **XUMAT**. Cross **MCT** D7 at 2500' or above (4.8%). At **MCT** D8 turn right to intercept **POL VOR** R221 (041°M) to **POL VOR**. Cross **POL** D16 at 4000' or above. Cross **POL** D9 at 5000'. Cross **POL VOR** at 5000'.	N57, N601, P18, P17/UP17 Northbound and for aircraft leaving controlled airspace.
POL 1Y 23L	Climb straight ahead at 12.33% or above (See Note 6). At **MCT** D3.2 turn right onto track 345°M towards **XUMAT**. Cross **MCT** D7 at 2500' or above (4.8%). At **MCT** D8 turn right to intercept **POL VOR** R221 (041°M) to **POL VOR**. Cross **POL** D16 at 4000' or above. Cross **POL** D9 at 5000'. Cross **POL VOR** at 5000'.	N57, N601, P18, P17/UP17 Northbound and for aircraft leaving controlled airspace.
POL 4S 05L†	Climb straight ahead. At not below 757' ALT (500' aal), but not before DER, adjust track onto **MCT VOR** R055 (See Note 6). At **MCT** D7 turn left to intercept **POL VOR** R182 (002°M) to **POL VOR**. Cross **POL** D12 at 4000' or above (4.27%). Cross **POL** D8 at 5000'. Cross **POL VOR** at 5000'.	N57, N601, P18, P17/UP17 Northbound and for aircraft leaving controlled airspace.
POL 1Z 05R	Climb straight ahead on **MCT VOR** R055 (See Note 6). At **MCT** D7 turn left to intercept **POL VOR** R182 (002°M) to **POL VOR**. Cross **POL** D12 at 4000' or above. Cross **POL** D8 at 5000'. Cross **POL VOR** at 5000'.	N57, N601, P18, P17/UP17 Northbound and for aircraft leaving controlled airspace.

OBSTACLE CLEARANCE - † RWY 23R/RWY 05L: Close in obstacles exist below 100' AAL and are not considered for procedure gradients.

GENERAL INFORMATION
1 SIDs reflect Noise Preferential Routeings. See EGCC AD 2.21 for Noise Abatement Procedures.
2 **No turns below 757' QNH (500' QFE).**
3 En-route cruising levels will be allocated after departure by 'Manchester Control'. **Do not climb above SID level until cleared by ATC.**
4 Callsign for RTF frequency used **when instructed** after take-off 'Manchester Control'. On first contact advise callsign/SID designator current altitude and cleared altitude.
5 Maximum 250KIAS below FL100 unless otherwise authorised.
6 **WARNING: RUNWAY 23L/05L. In the event of a missed approach on runway 23R/05R ATC may instruct aircraft which have departed from runway 23L/05L to make a LEFT turn in order to establish separation.**

CHANGE: NOTE 3. MAG VAR.

Manchester Standard Instrument Departure chart via Pole Hill
Courtesy of National Air Traffic Services

Emirates A380-861 (A6-EDC) departing London Heathrow runway 27 left
Shaun Grist

radio. Provided the receiver is in reasonable proximity to the transmitter, and not obstructed by buildings, hills and so on, the quality can be very good. However, if the line-of-sight is interrupted reception will be reduced or even eliminated altogether.

For this reason, hearing controllers' messages is simply not possible in many areas of the UK, most especially in hilly or mountainous regions. However, transmissions from aircraft are generally of good quality, especially from those at higher altitudes.

All frequencies allocated for aeronautical use are in Megahertz, grouped into three distinct and wide-ranging groups. The lowest frequency is 2 MHz, the highest 400 MHz. The frequency of a radio signal is measured in cycles per second; one cycle per second is known as a HERTZ, so named after a German physicist, Heinrich Rudolf Hertz, in the nineteenth century.

One thousand cycles per second is referred to as a KILO-hertz (kHz), and one million cycles per second is known as a MEGA-hertz (MHz). Thus, one thousand Kilohertz (kHz) is the same as one Megahertz (MHz). As an example, one popular frequency in the High Frequency range, used by flights crossing the North Atlantic, is '5649'. This is 5649 kHz or (more properly) 5.649 MHz.

High Frequency radio frequencies are also described as Shortwave, although most references use the term HF. They are used by flights over oceanic regions due to their particularly long range and are normally stated in Kilohertz (kHz) and therefore consist of four or five figures (e.g. 8864 or 10069). Receiver specifications normally state the range of frequencies in Megahertz (MHz) – in these cases the range falls between 8 and 11 MHz.

Aeronautical Frequency Bands

Three groups of frequencies are used in air traffic control:

- High Frequency or HF
- Very High Frequency or VHF
- Ultra High Frequency or UHF

High Frequency (Shortwave)

This system is used where it is necessary to pass messages over long distances. The frequency range is in groups between 2 MHz and 23 MHz, with other frequencies allocated for purposes other than aviation. HF has been used for decades for communicating with aircraft, even when messages were transmitted in Morse code. Today, an increasing number of aircraft use controller/pilot datalink communications, using satellite technology for making reports to ATC.

Very High Frequency (VHF)

All civil flights and certain military traffic use VHF for all types of communication over land, as the line-of-sight principle enables messages to be sent across distances of up to 150 miles. The frequencies range from 118 MHz to 136.975 MHz. The frequencies between 108 MHz and 117.975 MHz are used for ground-based navigation purposes. Some pilots, especially those on military flights, describe the VHF range as Victor frequencies.

Ultra High Frequency (UHF)

Military flights operating over land and adjoining sea areas transmit on frequencies in a range between 225 MHz and 400 MHz. This group is known as Ultra High Frequency or UHF, often known as 'Uniform' frequencies to pilots. However, if a military flight is using one of the civil routes it will normally use VHF.

Repeater Frequencies

Another group of frequencies (455.475-455.975 MHz Narrow Band FM) are used as repeater stations at airfields for use by ground operational staff who are able to listen to ATC instructions at the same time as communicating with each other. These frequencies are not normally available on a dedicated airband scanner, but are available with some of the more sophisticated sets.

Radio Frequency Information

It is comparatively easy to find information about radio frequencies used for ATC purposes. They are all freely available to the public, with civil frequencies listed on official websites.

In addition, most aviation bookshops publish information manuals specifically for airband listeners. Some radio navigation charts, as well as indicating routes through UK airspace, also contain frequency information, but it is generally easier and cheaper to find the details elsewhere – via the Internet, for example.

Another source of information is the Communications Supplements, published by the Royal Air Force or by Euronautical Limited. The RAF BINA edition (British Isles and North Atlantic) is particularly informative in respect of UK military airfields. They cover a great amount of detail about aviation procedures, as well as frequencies, but they are a little on the expensive side, although out of date issues can often be purchased for much less at air shows.

By far the easiest method, and completely free, is the official NATS website covering the United Kingdom Integrated Aeronautical Information Package (UKAIP). All the information about civilian (VHF) radio frequencies, UK airways and upper air routes and airports is available. Forthcoming changes are also posted on this site every month. Information on many other aspects of the civil aviation system can be accessed as well. Of course, the information only covers UK airspace.

For details, the NATS website is at www.nats-uk.ead-it.com. Click on the UK Aeronautical Information Package, and then select either the En route section or Airfields. Upper air routes and airways are under the ENR 3 section, together with radio frequencies, and each airfield and airport is also covered. UK airband handbooks are available from several pulishers. They include much more information than the official sources, including details for other European airports. Most of the current UK frequencies are listed in the appendices, although it is possible that some of these may change over time. They will, however, provide a good starting point for those new to the hobby.

4. What Can I Hear?

Most communications between control centres and aircraft are in respect of en route flights using the airways system or the high-level routes in upper airspace. As they cross the UK they will pass through several sectors, changing radio frequencies as they transfer from one sector to the next. Aircraft intending to land at one of the UK airfields will be handed on to the ATC unit at the destination airport, invariably when crossing a particular navigation fix at an agreed level. Those flights continuing beyond the UK will be handed over to controllers in one of the adjoining countries.

Messages between ATC and en route flights are often very brief, sometimes no more than an initial report to the sector controller followed by an acknowledgement, since most will be following an agreed flight plan. However, on the first contact with each ATC centre, the pilots will be given a clearance detailing the route the aircraft is expected to follow, so these radio frequencies used by sector controllers at the boundaries of UK airspace are invariably more interesting. Numerous agencies are involved in controlling or providing information to aircraft, using a wide range of different radio frequencies, and the listener can choose which aspects of the system are most suitable.

The parts of the service are:

Radar Control, where en route aircraft are under the control of an ATC unit.
Terminal Control, providing a control service to aircraft arriving at, or departing from, one of several airports in close proximity.
Airport Control, providing a service to arrivals, departures, and low-level overflights.
North Atlantic Clearances, where westbound oceanic flights request clearances to enter the North Atlantic.
Flight Information Services, providing a range of services to flights outside controlled airspace.
Meteorological and other information, broadcast from individual airports or covering groups of airports.
Company Messages, used by airlines and their pilots to relay information concerning the flights.
Distress and Diversion, providing a service to aircraft which are lost or experiencing an emergency.

These are described in more detail later.

Cathay Pacific Cargo B747 on finals to Manchester runway 23 right Author

Listening to an airband radio for the first time may be confusing, as the messages are often quite short and spoken quickly, using unfamiliar terms which cannot be recognised.

However, over time the messages become easier to understand and in many cases, for each particular frequency, they will be found to be fairly repetitive. The most common, and busiest, transmissions are between pilots and controllers, perhaps locally around airfields, or en route for high level traffic under the control of an area or terminal control centre.

En Route Traffic

The United Kingdom and Ireland provide the main gateway to the North Atlantic for European air traffic, with a significant proportion of traffic overflying the region at high levels. These flights, as well as internal UK traffic, are controlled from Area Control Centres at Swanwick, Prestwick or Shannon on VHF or UHF frequencies. As flights cross the country they pass from one sector to the next and each time this occurs there will be a frequency change given by the controller. Most of the current published frequencies

Stansted Visual Control Room with
Electronic Flight Progress Strips Display
Courtesy of National Air Traffic Services

are listed in geographical groups in the Appendices.

Most of the frequencies within this category will be transmitted on the 'offset' principle, which is described later. Traffic at high and lower levels may be under the jurisdiction of different teams of controllers, as the sectors are split vertically in many parts of the UK. This means that flights passing overhead may be using two different radio frequencies.

Terminal Manoeuvring Areas (TMAs)

Where a number of civil airports are grouped together (as, for example, around London) and the traffic density is high, arrivals and departures, as well as aircraft in transit, are controlled by a special unit created to manage the complex flight patterns. TMA airspace usually has a lower limit of around 3,000 feet and an upper limit (in the case of the London TMA) of FL245.

'Volmet' Broadcasts

There are four VHF frequencies which are used to continuously broadcast a variety of information for UK and some continental airports. This system is known as 'VOLMET'.

LONDON VOLMET MAIN - Frequency 135.375
LONDON VOLMET SOUTH - Frequency 128.6
LONDON VOLMET NORTH - Frequency 126.6
SCOTTISH VOLMET – Frequency 125.725

Two High Frequency services are also used for Volmet. These are:

SHANNON VOLMET (Broadcast from Ballygirreen Radio Station, near Shannon) – Most European airports are covered by this service, on high frequency radio, for eastbound transatlantic traffic.

ROYAL AIR FORCE VOLMET - This service provides details for all European military airfields which are used by the RAF.

Details of the coverage of Volmet broadcasts are given in the appendices.

All Volmet broadcasts are compiled from pre-recorded voice segments which cover all possible combinations of weather conditions. These are automatically linked together by computer to give a very realistic continuous message for each airport covered. The broadcasts are continuous throughout the day and night with automatic updating as new information is received.

Automatic Terminal Information Services (ATIS)

Many of the larger airfields in the UK broadcast details of local weather conditions on a continuous basis on specific frequencies; these are published on the NATS AIS website (mentioned earlier) and in the appendices. At smaller airfields, where the use of a dedicated frequency is not justified, the weather and other relevant details are passed, on request, by ATC personnel to individual flights.

As airfields become increasingly busy the 'air time' taken by controllers in reading out weather details reaches a level whereby an alternative method becomes essential; a separate frequency is then introduced for the continuous broadcast of local conditions.

Stansted Visual Control Room with Electronic Flight Progress Strips Display
Courtesy of National Air Traffic Services

ATIS messages are always identified by a letter (for example 'This is Birmingham Information Hotel'). The broadcast will continue on a repetitive basis until one of the aspects included in the message is changed. The revised information will then be broadcast in an updated format prefixed with the next letter of the alphabet – in this case 'Birmingham Information India'.

When pilots first contact the airfield they are able to identify the information they have obtained on their second radio by reference to the particular letter - for example, 'Golf Charlie Delta we have information India'. This confirms to the controller that the pilot has received the latest ATIS broadcast.

Gliders, Microlights, Hang-Gliders, Balloons and Parachutists

Each of these categories of flight has a dedicated VHF radio frequency which enables pilots to communicate with each other and with their bases.

These are:

129.900Mhz   Gliders, Hang Gliders and Balloons
130.300Mhz   Parachutists

London City Visual Control Room
Courtesy of National Air Traffic Services

Information and Advisory Services

Flights outside controlled or regulated airspace may request an information service on one of the dedicated VHF frequencies for London or Scottish airspace, using the callsigns London Information and Scottish Information. These services are limited to basic information regarding other traffic, facilities at airfields and so on, but remaining clear of other aircraft and terrain clearance is always the pilot's responsibility. The service is not backed up by radar, and there is no obligation on pilots to use the service.

Other types of service are available from controllers and flight information service officers based at airfields, offering basic information, traffic information, a deconfliction service and procedural control, but again, the pilots are always responsible for avoiding other traffic and for terrain clearance.

Local Airfields

Most UK airfields, with the exception of small landing strips, have one or more radio frequencies for handling traffic arriving, departing, or moving around on the ground. They also cater for low level transiting flights. Controllers in the Visual Control Room, using the 'Tower' frequency, handle aircraft landing, taking off or flying within the visual circuit. The 'Approach' controller, usually assisted by radar, will deal with flights away from the airfield itself, as well as inbound and outbound traffic.

Busier airfields may be provided with separate 'Ground' and 'Clearance Delivery' frequencies, dealing with the movement of all traffic, including vehicles, on the runways and taxiways, and also flight-plan clearances. Most military airfields also have a range of VHF frequencies for those flights which are not provided with UHF radio. The larger complex airports, such as Heathrow, have several other frequencies, each allocated to specific tasks within the airport structure, enabling the airfield to operate smoothly and safely, although several now use datalink to pass route-clearance messages directly to the flight deck, reducing air time and the possibility of errors and misunderstandings.

Fire Service Vehicles
Airport fire service vehicles operate on frequency 121.6 MHz (VHF) when dealing with emergencies within the airfield boundary.

North Atlantic Oceanic Clearances
Before an aircraft is permitted to enter the airspace of the North Atlantic it must obtain air traffic control authorisation from the Oceanic Area Control Centre at Prestwick, Scotland. Clearances are negotiated between pilots and controllers, using dedicated VHF radio frequencies, or datalink communications, while the aircraft is in flight over the UK or the surrounding sea areas.

Checking runway equipment, London Stanstead
Courtesy of National Air Traffic Services

British Airways B747-436 (G-CIVM) departing London Heathrow runway 27 left Shaun Grist

Most flights to the American continent pass through UK airspace in the late morning and early afternoon, communicating on one of two dedicated frequencies. However, the introduction of datalink communications has resulted in a dramatic reduction in the number of aircraft using the VHF voice system. Currently, around two thirds of the transatlantic traffic now receive their clearances via VHF datalink and as a result the number of voice messages is now far lower than previously. At one time, three frequencies were in use but this has been reduced to two. Some flights, of course, can still be heard on VHF. These may be non-standard flights, pilots with particular queries or aircraft not fitted with datalink capability.

The two frequencies currently in use are 123.950 MHz (normally used by aircraft registered in America or Canada) and 127.650 MHz (used by aircraft registered in Europe). Oceanic clearance requests, and ATC approvals, are sent via transmitters at Mangersta (Outer Hebrides), Grantham (Lincolnshire), Dundonald Hill (Scotland) and Davidstow Moor (Cornwall). Unless your receiver is located in a position within reasonable distance from one of these transmitters the controller will not normally be heard on an airband receiver.

Airports close to the oceanic boundary are provided with local transmitters which enable the flight crew to obtain their clearance while still on the ground, and aircraft out of range of the VHF stations may use HF radio.

Distress and Diversion

Pilots who require urgent assistance – for example, unsure of their position, with engine trouble or any other emergency situation – can contact the Distress and Diversion unit at the control centres at Swanwick or Prestwick on the international emergency frequencies of 121.500 MHz (VHF) or 243.000 MHz (UHF). Aircraft which are already under the control of an air traffic control unit will usually report their problem to the controller on the frequency which they are currently using; the distress frequencies are normally used by aircraft outside regulated airspace.

Two callsigns are available, Mayday, Mayday, Mayday and Pan Pan, Pan Pan, Pan Pan. These cover two levels of emergency -

Mayday is for flights in real distress, whereas the lower level of emergency, Pan, is for flights which need assistance or guidance without the urgency of a full scale emergency. Pilots can often be heard on the distress frequency simulating emergencies with the callsign 'Practise Pan - Practise Pan - Practise Pan'. This gives pilots and controllers an opportunity to practise real life situations without the urgency of real time situations. The position of an aircraft using one of the distress frequencies is presented to controllers through an auto triangulation system which is effective over a large part of the UK.

B757 of Thomas Cook taxying at Manchester *Author*

Company Frequencies

Airlines and their pilots often need to communicate while a flight is in progress, and for this purpose a number of company frequencies have been allocated within the VHF range. These 'flight regularity' messages usually concern passenger requirements, medical assistance, technical queries, times of departure and arrival and so on, and are transmitted using a second radio on the flight deck.

Most of the larger airlines have one or more dedicated frequencies, often within the range between 129.00 and 132.00Mhz, and also between 136.00 and 137.00Mhz. The smaller companies usually route messages through an agency organisation, such as Servisair, with bases at most airports.

Singapore A380-841 (9V-SKD) departing London Heathrow runway 27 left
Shaun Grist

5. Choosing a Scanner

Newcomers to the hobby of airband listening often make the mistake of believing that the more expensive the receiver the better it will perform. This is simply not the case. In fact, some of the best models on the market are at the lower end of the price range. This is because the more sophisticated versions are not dedicated airband scanners but instead cover a wide range of frequencies and contain many features the airband listener may never use.

In the last ten years, more and more multi-purpose scanners have come onto the market, and while these are undoubtedly very advanced, they often do not produce results which are any better than ten or twenty-year-old models. Some of the original sets from the early 1990s have such a good reputation that they are difficult to come by on the second-hand market.

A few pertinent questions about the specification for a particular model will help the listener to reach a decision, as it is not always evident from advertisements exactly what is being offered. Most aviation enthusiasts only need to have a simple approach to the subject.

This may be summarised as follows:

Does it cover the range of frequencies that I need?
Are there any gaps in the range of frequencies?
How many memories does it have?
Are the memories in 'banks'?
Does it have lots of other frequencies that I will never use?
Can it be fine tuned in steps of 5kHz or less?
Is it battery or mains operated, or both?

Each of these aspects will be examined in this chapter.

Radio Modes

The radio transmission mode employed for aeronautical use is Amplitude Modulation or AM. The alternative system, FM is not used. AM is a method of transmitting radio waves where the carrier wave strength (the

Aero Svit B737-4Q8 (UR-VVP) departing Milan Bergamo
Shaun Grist

amplitude) is regularly varied (modulated) by an electric signal.

These regular changes against the background deliberately change an electromagnetic wave so that information can be transmitted. AM was the first system to be used for radio transmissions, especially for Morse code. Signals which are AM also create extra frequencies which are known as sidebands, both upper and lower, and it is one of these, upper sideband, which is used for High Frequency (HF) transmissions for traffic crossing oceanic regions. The lower sideband and the carrier wave frequency are both omitted. This process results in improved efficiency, since a considerable amount of the AM signal is taken up by the carrier wave. However, a specially designed receiver is essential for single sideband HF transmissions.

Frequency modulation (which is only used by ground staff at airports) varies the frequency of the signal. If the frequency modulation occurs over a limited range (usually around 3 kHz above and 3 kHz below the carrier wave) it is described as Narrow FM. Conversely, if the range is greater than a normal AM signal, it is said to be Wideband FM. Airband scanners do not normally have the facility for Narrow FM.

Frequencies

Most airband listeners are interested in civil air traffic control transmissions, as the messages are frequent, easier to understand and follow a basic structure which only changes occasionally. For this purpose, the VHF frequencies range from 118.000MHz to 136.975MHz in 'steps' of 25kHz, in other words each frequency is separated from the next by 25kHz. For example, 132.000, 132.025, 132.050, 132.075, 132.100, 132.125 and so on.

In an increasing number of cases, the 25kHz spacing has been further sub-divided into 8.33kHz steps, increasing the number of available channels. When these were originally introduced in Europe they were distinguished from the traditional system ('frequencies') by the use of the word 'channels'. This requirement was dropped in

Steepletone SAB2006 airband receiver
Waters and Stanton

November 2005 and replaced by new procedures which only use the word 'frequencies'.

The correct method in use today requires that for both systems all six digits are spoken as frequencies, the only exception being when the last two digits are zero, in which case only the first four are spoken.

For example:
133.975 is spoken as *'frequency one three three decimal nine seven five'*

132.005 is spoken as *'frequency one three two decimal zero zero five'*

129.700 is spoken as *'frequency one two nine decimal seven'*

A further point about the 8.33 system concerns radiotelephony procedures. It would obviously be too cumbersome for a controller to use the full frequency in ATC messages, so for this purpose they are rounded up or down. *This means that the frequency spoken by controllers is not the same as the frequency used to transmit the message.*

For example:
135.00833 is spoken as *'one three five decimal zero one zero'*

135.01666 is spoken as *'one three five decimal zero one five'*

Also, where a 25kHz frequency and an 8.33kHz frequency are the same, the 8.33 frequency has 5kHz added to distinguish one from the other.

Under both systems, whole number frequencies are the same but as the radio operating principles are different there must be no confusion between the two.

For example,
134.000 is spoken as *'frequency one three four decimal zero'* (25kHz steps)

134.000 is spoken as *'frequency one three four decimal zero zero five'* (8.33kHz steps)

However, this does not mean that in order to listen to the 8.33 frequencies it is essential to have a receiver with these specific steps. If you are aware of the actual channel being used (they can be found in many of the sources available today, or by listening to aircraft being transferred from one sector to the next) it will be possible to tune the receiver close to the actual frequency provided the receiver has steps of 5 kHz or less. The frequency can then be stored in the memory for future use.

It is only in the search mode that 8.33 kHz spacing become essential, but this is a relatively unimportant drawback since it is fairly easy to identify frequencies and channels. Most transmissions operate at around 5 kHz above or below the published frequency and can be received quite adequately on most modern scanners. So, for example, tuning to a channel of 132.083 by entering 132.080 or 132.085 will be perfectly adequate.

Military frequencies

For those in areas of the UK with significant military activity, a scanner with UHF frequencies can be considered. Many models have both VHF and UHF. However, the number of military transmissions on the UHF band is far less than is usually experienced with civilian air traffic on VHF. This is partly because there are many more available frequencies and partly because military aviation transmissions are allocated frequencies not only related to the location of the flight but also to the function of the flight – in other words, the kind of task the aircraft is performing often determines the frequency to be used irrespective of the area in which it is working. Also, military flights

Icom IC-A110 airband scanner
Waters and Stanton

Icom IC-R22 airband scanner
Waters and Stanton

tend to operate mostly during weekday periods; the number of flights taking place during the night and at weekends is very much reduced.

VHF and UHF
Airband Receivers

To summarise, do not assume from technical specifications, full of detailed statistics, that the scanner is capable of receiving virtually all that the airband enthusiast can ever require. Although a particular model might well be superb it does not necessarily mean that the frequencies cover the entire airband range, or that performance in the airband channels give the best results. Some sets are said to cover 'VHF and UHF airbands' whereas in fact there can be gaps in the frequencies which can actually be received, particularly in the military range.

Sometimes the same model receiver produced by the same manufacturer at different times may have an updated range of frequencies on the later model. Also sets on sale abroad may not be equipped to the same standard as UK models since the sale of receivers with airband frequencies is illegal in many parts of the world, so beware of suspicious special offers. Some models also have frequency steps that are not used for airband frequencies – for example, a step of 6.25kHz is of no use for VHF or UHF listening.

The specialist UK companies do give good advice when choosing a scanner and they are happy to talk through individual requirements, but some of the more general suppliers may not fully understand the way in which the system works and therefore can give misleading information. Try to be clear about what the new purchase will actually do and check with the seller on your specific requirements.

High Frequency (Short Wave)

The transmissions on the HF group of frequencies can only be received on a certain type of receiver, and because the principles involved are quite different from those used for VHF and UHF the subject is dealt with in a separate chapter. There are now several handheld receivers on the market which cover all three aeronautical ranges. However, experience indicates that these rarely, if ever, give results which compare with dedicated equipment.

Offset Frequency Spacing

Most airband transmissions operate at frequencies which are 'stepped' (i.e. separated) by 25 kHz, the normal spacing used in aviation voice transmissions, although more and more now have spacings of 8.33kHz. Under the 25kHz system, in order to give increased range, ATC messages are often transmitted from more than one location. To avoid interference between the different transmitters the actual frequency being used may be slightly higher or lower than published. The actual transmission can be 2.5, 5.0 or 7.5 kHz higher or lower than the official promulgated frequency. These are known as 'offsets'.

Maycom AR 108 airband scanner
Waters and Stanton

If your scanner is receiving signals from a transmitter operating on one of these offset frequencies it is possible that reception will be improved if the receiver can be tuned to a frequency slightly higher or slightly lower than the published one, so that it matches more closely the actual transmission. If the signals are strong, the offset will not have any effect on reception, but if the signals are weak (due perhaps to the distance between the receiver and the transmitter) the slight difference can improve matters considerably.

For example, if messages on a published frequency of 133.600 were being transmitted simultaneously from four separate sites, the actual frequencies being used would be:

133.5925; 133.5975; 133.6025; 133.6075

These four frequencies are each separated by 5kHz. This is why there can be a positive improvement in the quality of reception if the receiver can be tuned in 5kHz steps or even less. Some of the latest scanners can be programmed to step down as low as 1 kHz, therefore the user can select any frequency across the entire range with an accuracy of

1 kHz. An alternative use for this feature is to 'tone down' a particularly strong and distorted signal from a transmitter located near to the receiver.

Squelch

Virtually all VHF or UHF receivers are provided with a 'squelch' control, a device which is used to eliminate the continuous background noise which would otherwise be heard between messages. However, there are some second-hand sets around that do not have this feature so it is worth checking. The squelch control is usually operated by a rotary switch which eliminates background noise and interference. The most sensitive reception is obtained when the squelch switch is only just beyond the point where the background noise stops. Without this facility reception is spoiled by 'hiss' and interference. In addition, the search and scan functions will not operate while any background noise is present. Also, tape recording with a voice-activated recorder is difficult, if not impossible.

Alinco DJ-X3 airband scanner
Waters and Stanton

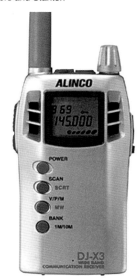

Repeater Frequencies

A further area of interest for the airband listener is the repeater frequencies used at airports. These are Personal Mobile Radio channels in the Narrow FM range which enable airport staff (ground engineers, fire crews, vehicle drivers, police, and so on) to listen to messages from Air Traffic Control and aircraft. They operate on the duplex system, that is, the base station and the mobile transceiver send and receive messages on different frequencies. Few airband scanners are provided with NFM mode, therefore tuning in to these channels will not be possible, but this should not deter one from purchasing a particular receiver since the additional interest is very limited. Frequencies are usually in the range 453.0000 to 456.0000 MHz range. Details for individual airports may be found in specialist scanning handbooks.

Memorising and Scanning

Most modern airband receivers are capable of storing a number of frequencies, ranging from one hundred to a few thousand. This feature allows frequencies chosen by the listener to be stored in the receiver's memory, which is then 'scanned' for any active channels. If the scan detects a transmission the receiver will remain on that frequency until the transmission ends, after which the scan will resume.

Most scanners have a delay feature which allows the receiver to remain on one frequency for several seconds before restarting the scan. This allows for the fact that there can be a short interval between one transmission and the next. Some receivers can be programmed to adjust the delay at the end of a transmission between two and ten seconds. The listener can also set the receiver to remain on one particular frequency indefinitely by selecting the 'hold' option.

Another feature is the sub-division of the memory into 'banks' of ten or twenty channels. This permits the storage and scanning of separate groups of frequencies according to the needs of the user. Each bank can be scanned individually or they can be

Alinco DJ-X7 airband scanner
Waters and Stanton

linked together; therefore this facility has obvious advantages. Naturally, the ability to store frequencies has no effect on the quality of reception of the individual receiver - it merely makes the selection of frequencies much more convenient and relieves the listener of the chore of entering separate channels each time they are needed.

Searching

The search facility is quite different from the scan mode. Searching allows the receiver to check through all the available frequencies, not just those in the memory, stopping whenever a signal is detected. This can be a voice transmission or just interference. The search will depend on the channel steps programmed into the receiver – for example if the spacing is set to 25kHz the receiver will search in increments of 25kHz, missing out, for example, 8.33 channels. Alternatively, if it is set to 5kHz steps it will check every 5kHz.

The search facility can often be set to operate only between two frequencies set by the listener. If for example the listener wished to check the frequencies between 130.000MHz and 133.000MHz, these two parameters would be entered before the search was commenced.

If a frequency of interest is detected this can be added directly to the memory. The ability to 'delay' or to 'hold', described under 'Scanning', also applies to the 'Search' mode.

During a search or scan, the process will stop at any signal it detects, and it is often the case that some of those signals will not be of interest to the listener - for example, continuous weather transmissions, airfield information transmissions, or simply interference. To deal with this, most sets with scan and search features will be capable of locking out these. If the scan or search stops at an unwanted frequency the 'pass' or 'lock-out' key is pressed. The search (or scan) then continues, the locked-out frequencies subsequently being ignored by the receiver. Any frequency which has been locked out can be brought back into the circuit by pressing the same key again.

Priority Channel

When a receiver is operating in either Scan or Search mode, the user may choose to select one or two channels of particular interest. This means that these 'priority' channels will be checked at regular intervals (usually every few seconds) while the receiver is scanning a range of memorised channels, or searching through a sequence of frequencies. If a signal is detected the receiver will remain on the priority channel until the end of the message. It will then revert to the search or scan mode as appropriate.

Some listeners may have one or two special interest channels - for example the emergency frequency of 121.5 (VHF) or 243.0 (UHF) which is only used very occasionally – but apart from this kind of use the priority channel is unlikely to be of particular value to the airband listener and, in any case, such attributes do nothing to enhance the receiver's performance.

Power Supply

Most airband receivers can be powered from the mains supply, through the use of an appropriate adapter. Hand-held scanners are also battery powered, either by the normal dry cells or by the rechargeable type. Take care when choosing an adapter, especially with the polarity and the voltage. The receiver can be permanently damaged if these are incorrectly set. Most specialist outlets can supply a mains adapter suitable for a particular product but sometimes it will be necessary to obtain a separate adapter from an independent supplier, in which case care is needed to make sure the unit is compatible with the receiver. It is advisable to purchase such items only from reputable outlets as it is possible to damage the receiver by the use of unsuitable equipment.

In some cases, the receiver can only be operated by using the manufacturer's own power unit. These can be quite costly, so check before buying. Some 'base' stations which are designed to be used at a fixed location, may not have provision for internal batteries. However, this can be overcome by purchasing an external battery compartment and fitting the required number of batteries. For example, a base station receiver which operates on a 12 volt supply can also be run by eight AA batteries of 1.5 volts each.

Icom IC-R5 airband scanner
Waters and Stanton

Icom IC-R20 airband scanner
Waters and Stanton

Normal batteries are expensive for everyday use, especially if the receiver is used mainly as a base station in the home or in a car. Rechargeable batteries are very economical in use, once the initial cost of purchasing the recharging unit and at least two sets of batteries has been met. These batteries can be recharged hundreds of times at a very low cost, although their 'life' in some cases can be quite low – perhaps a few hours – so they are not the most suitable type for sets used almost continuously. However, the higher power versions, although more expensive initially, do have much longer lives. Some receivers are provided with the means for recharging the batteries while still in the set. The recharging unit also serves as a power supply source which operates the receiver directly. The recharger,

therefore, operates the scanner when it is in use, and continues to recharge the batteries when the receiver is switched off.

A scanner which has a connection for an external power source can be used with an adapter which can be connected to the cigarette lighter socket of a vehicle. The adapter must be switched to the correct output voltage appropriate to the receiver, and it is also important to ensure that the polarity of the connections are matched to the set. Car power adapters are usually provided with a reversible polarity socket, so the 'plus' and 'minus' connection to the receiver can easily be fitted incorrectly. Care must be taken to match the connections correctly so that the set is not damaged.

Antenna Connections

Virtually all popular airband scanners are provided with an antenna which is connected to the set by a BNC type fitting, or, occasionally, a PL259 fitting. The BNC type is neater and smaller and therefore less cumbersome for the smaller receiver, while the PL259 is a heavier unit. Most, but not all, modern scanners are now provided with the BNC type of antenna connection. Both types can be used with antennas or receivers because each one can be converted by the use of the appropriate adaptor. When connecting to an external antenna, co-axial cable suitable for airband frequencies must be used.

Suitable adapters for converting from one type of connector to another are available from most radio equipment suppliers. Both BNC and PL 259 connections are available in 'solderless' versions. One or two models have uncommon antenna connections but adapters are available from airband radio specialists. Some base-station receivers are supplied without an antenna – the purchaser is expected to select a suitable antenna system most appropriate to the set, bearing in mind the location where it will be used, the proximity of transmitters, and so on. Of course, any receiver with one of the usual connections can be fitted with more than one antenna – perhaps one for mobile use and one for use as a base station.

Yupiteru MVT-7100 airband scanner
Waters and Stanton

Low Cost Receivers

There are some inexpensive airband receivers on the market that do not have the sophisticated features described earlier, but may nevertheless be adequate for someone who is starting out in the field of airband listening. These receivers use the traditional 'continuous' tuning method used in the old fashioned domestic radio receiver which operates by simply shifting a pointer across a waveband dial, covering the full range of VHF frequencies very quickly.

Some people may be understandably hesitant about spending perhaps two hundred pounds or more on a receiver when they are unsure about the quality of the messages they are likely to receive in their area. Also, being a new hobby, they may decide to 'test the water' before reaching a decision on whether to move up-market into the realms of the sophisticated sets described earlier. However, these models are limited and the selection of individual channels is not possible, and in practice signals from more than one transmission may be detected at the same point on the dial. Inexpensive receivers tend to suffer badly from local interference, with unwanted signals breaking through and obliterating aeronautical transmissions. These sets are, of course, simply a taster for the newcomer and their ability to give good results is very limited. Nevertheless they can sometimes be perfectly adequate for the occasional listener on a low budget, especially in an area of strong signals.

Secondhand Receivers

All the specialist airband radio outlets are able to offer good quality scanners on the second hand market, often taken in part exchange for a more sophisticated models. They are also advertised in radio magazines and on the Internet, but a checklist of questions is worthwhile before making a decision. Some very good bargains can be found, especially where the equipment has been given as a gift and may never have been used.

These sources are ideal for the first-time buyer, provided sensible questions are asked concerning frequencies, frequency steps, and so on, as described earlier. Some of the most reliable scanners are now only available on the secondhand market. Most of these are covered in the appendices. Most of the airband radio suppliers listed in the appendices offer a selection of used models, each with a three-month or six-month guarantee.

6. Antennas

Thirty-five years' experience in VHF and UHF airband listening has resulted in one definite conclusion – a simple low-cost antenna is as good as, and often out performs, more expensive models, and reports from other enthusiasts over the years have confirmed this. If the listener is fortunate to be in a location close to a transmitter site then the choice of antenna may not be that important, but in other situations the range and quality of reception will be improved considerably with an external antenna.

VHF and UHF transmissions are only effective if there is a reasonable line of sight between the source and the receiver. Messages from high-level aircraft can usually be heard at a distance of at least 100 miles if this condition is satisfied, but those from the ground are far less reliable, usually limited to 30 or 40 miles where the area between the two is reasonably uninterrupted. At airports, transmissions are strong and reception is usually quite good even with a simple whip type aerial, but for *en route* flights the picture

is often disappointing. In some parts of the country, listeners only hear the occasional aircraft and never receive ATC transmissions so interest can quickly evaporate. Most scanners, however, will benefit from the addition of an external antenna, and even simple aerials fitted directly to the receiver can be improved quite easily.

In many cases, it does not make sense to ignore the benefits of an external aerial system, especially as these can be obtained for a fraction of the cost of the receiver. Even if you are in an area where there is good reception, significant improvements in hearing more distant traffic will make the small investment worthwhile. There are two kinds of simple antenna – one which is capable of receiving signals from every direction in equal strength, known as 'omni-

Air Nav Radar Box with antenna and laptop computer
Image generated by AirNav Systems RadarBox – www.airnavsystems.com

SIMPLE DIPOLE ANTENNAS Dimensions of Elements (in millimetres)			
	120MHz	125MHz	130MHz	135MHz

	120MHz	125MHz	130MHz	135MHz
A	595	570	550	525
B	50	50	50	50
C	595	570	550	525

Dimensions for VHF airband antennas
Author (see diagrams)

directional', where the elements of the aerial are vertical; and the other which is designed to concentrate the received signals, and amplify them, from one particular point, (probably an *en route* transmitter or an airport) so that the strongest possible signal is heard. These are known as 'directional' aerials.

Airband antennas only need to be of a basic design and are well within the capabilities of most airband listeners. Alternatively, VHF aerials designed for commercial radio reception are not expensive and can be easily modified for airband use. Remember that the same comments apply to antennas as to receivers – spending more and more money often has no significant effect on performance. Good all round results can often be achieved with the simplest homemade systems made up from discarded television or radio aerials at minimal cost. VHF and UHF transmissions operate on the 'line-of-sight' principle, similar to television and FM radio. Therefore, an expensive receiver used in a location where there is no line-of-sight to the transmitter will give poor results, even with a good antenna. Alternatively, a basic receiver, located in a suitable position close to a transmitter, will usually perform well even with the simplest of antennas.

Antenna 'systems' are a combination of a number of separate component parts, covering the overall design and location of the antenna, its installation, the cable feed to the receiver, the various connections, amplifiers, and, of course, the receiver itself. The omni-directional type of antenna will be quite adequate in areas of good overall airband coverage, with ATC transmitters within 50 miles or so, and with a reasonable line of sight. In other situations, where the line of sight is obstructed or the antenna is too far away from the transmitter, there can be some benefit from a directional type of antenna which can at least be pointed towards the airport or transmitter. Directional systems, however, suffer from reduced signal strength from other sources that are not in line with the antenna (aircraft, for example). It is impossible to give positive advice for every situation since so much depends upon the local circumstances and the relative positions of aircraft, airfields, transmitters and other features likely to affect reception.

It is possible to gain a significant improvement in signal quality by relatively small adjustments in the position of an external antenna or a handheld set fitted with its own aerial. Surprisingly, positioning a handheld scanner close to an internal wall surface can often improve reception considerably. In many cases, reception is better in this position than when next to a window.

A simple but effective VHF antenna
Courtesy of Moonraker (UK) Limited

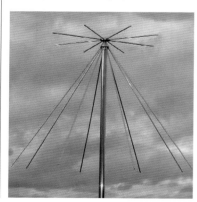

Antenna Design

There are two basic types of simple antennas:

Single element vertical designs, often referred to as Marconi type aerials.

Dipoles, consisting of two separate halves of a vertical element, which act together as a single antenna.

Marconi Type Antennas

This is a single perpendicular antenna, designed to resonate at a particular frequency according to the length of the element, using the ground or metal radials. For portable systems, a car roof acts as the 'ground'. To design a simple antenna for VHF airband, take the average frequency between the lowest (118.000MHz) and the highest (137.000MHz). This is around 127.000MHz. However, most *en route* frequencies are towards the top end of the scale, so a more sensible figure to use would be 130.000.

The length of the element (in metres) is determined by dividing the speed of radio waves (300 million metres per second, the same as the speed of light) by the frequency in hertz. So, for example, for the frequency 130 MHz (130 million hertz), the calculation would be 300,000,000 divided by 130,000,000 (or 300 divided by 130), which equals 2.308 metres. In practice, however, effective results can be achieved by using an element which is a quarter of the wavelength, or 577mm. In addition, for technical reasons, it is normal practice to reduce this by 5 per cent; therefore the final length is 548mm, or 21.5 inches.

Antenna lengths for any other frequency can be calculated in the same way. The frequencies used for aeronautical communication range between 118 MHz at the lowest end, on VHF, to 400 MHz at the highest on UHF. By using the formula for single element vertical antennas the lengths of the elements vary from 600 millimetres to 175 millimetres. This simple formula can also be applied to handheld scanners. Try fitting a telescopic metal aerial in place of the usual short black 'rubber duck' type normally

A simple but effective VHF antenna
Courtesy of Moonraker (UK) Limited

supplied with most scanners. Extending the aerial to 550mm often produces a better result.

Do not worry too much about being accurate about the exact measurements. The final result will be influenced to a far greater extent by other factors (such as the height of the antenna, good clean connections and so on) so the dimensions should be looked upon as no more than a guide. For most purposes an antenna suitable for the middle of the range of frequencies will usually be adequate. The addition of some kind of metal 'ground' at its base, for example a car roof, a square piece of strong wire mesh or lengths of tube, may improve the signal but often the difference in quality is negligible.

Dipoles

The most popular 'do-it-yourself' antenna is the dipole, which consists of two single elements, again mounted vertically, one above the other, with the centre core of the co-axial cable connected to the upper element and the outer braid connected to the lower element. The two elements are both the same length as the single type described earlier. This type does not require a ground to be effective, but the elements must be insulated from each other. If the antenna is

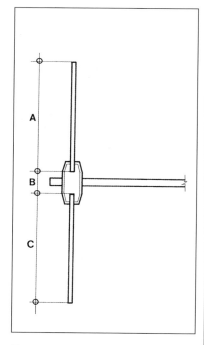

Easy to make, this simple dipole airband antenna is very effective.
Author

to be mounted internally – for example, in a roof space – this can be achieved by fixing the elements to a timber backboard. Alternatively, a suitable cable connection box can be purchased from aerial suppliers.

A ready-made dipole can be made from an FM radio antenna, which will have elements longer than required for airband. They simply need to be reduced in length to the desired dimensions. FM antennas are available from most good radio dealers. For receiving both VHF and UHF transmissions, two Marconi type antennas, or alternatively two dipole antennas, can be erected side by side in a location as high as possible, with separate co-axial down-leads to the receiver. The two antennas must be cut to length for the respective UHF and VHF frequencies, and the leads will have to be switched from one antenna to the other according to the station being received.

Many designs of airband antenna are available from radio dealers and specialist manufacturers, and some readers may prefer to purchase one direct rather than bother with making one. However, do not assume that because these simple antennas are relatively easy and cheap to make that they are less effective than other antennas advertised and sold by specialist companies. Experience shows that they are very efficient and can be just as good as those which can be purchased readymade.

Folded Dipoles

A marginally more efficient version of the dipole antenna is the type known as a 'folded' dipole in which a normal dipole design is provided with an additional element which connects the two extreme ends, resulting in an antenna with slightly improved capabilities when compared to the normal dipole. Folded dipoles are efficient over a wider range of frequencies than the single dipole. This type of antenna can often be seen around airports and at police stations. The dimensions of the two arms are calculated by using the same formula as given previously. Often, however, the improvement is minimal and not worth the effort.

Nests of Dipoles

For complete coverage of a wide range of frequencies capable of handling VHF and UHF, it is possible to link together a series of antennas of different lengths, cut according to the frequencies required, and fed to the receiver with a single co-axial lead. The idea with this kind of antenna is that each frequency in the entire range is catered for by the different lengths of the elements, resulting in better all round coverage. This kind of antenna has become known as a 'nest of dipoles'. They are available commercially but it is also possible to make one at home for internal use and reports as to its effectiveness are very favourable.

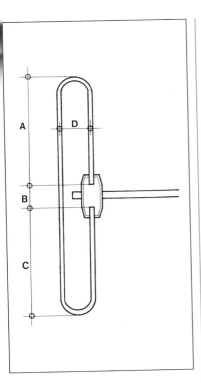

A

D

B

C

The folded dipole antenna may achieve a marginal improvement over the simple dipole Author

If it is desired to listen only to one range of frequencies (VHF airband for example) it might not be worth the time and expense to provide a multiple dipole type of antenna, since the range of frequencies is relatively short and reception may not be significantly improved by such a system. However, there is no way of knowing how a particular design will work unless it is tried under working conditions.

Mobile Antennas

Most airband listeners will want to spend at least some of their time listening to aircraft at airports or in other areas away from their home base. Often the built-in aerial will be adequate, but performance will undoubtedly be improved with a separate external antenna. The most popular type is a single element aerial with a magnetic base which is attached to the roof of a vehicle, the metal roof acting as a ground screen. Another type of portable aerial consists of a length of FM ribbon antenna, cut to the correct dimensions, with a cable connection for the receiver. This can be used in any location but is particularly useful when away from home as it can be folded away and easily carried.

Active Antenna Systems

An active antenna is one which uses electrical power for its operation. They are often much smaller than conventional antennas and can therefore be used in smaller spaces. The power supply is provided from a battery or through a transformer from the mains. Active antennas are particularly useful in areas of poor reception and where the use of an external antenna is not possible. Unfortunately, it is very difficult to assess the efficiency of each design without having direct experience in your particular location. Sometimes the results will be good but at other times may be poor. It might be possible to persuade your supplier to agree to refund the cost of the antenna if it is found to be unsuitable. Based on experience, and taking account of reports from users, it seems that these designs can be disappointing.

Cables

The cable (known as the feeder) used with antennas suitable for UHF and VHF aeronautical transmissions is a 50 ohm co-axial type, thinner than television aerial cable. It consists of a central copper core surrounded by insulation and covered by a woven wire screen which is then surrounded by a plastic outer cover. TV cable is 75 ohms and therefore does not match airband transmissions. The correct antenna cables for airband use are types UR43 or UR67, both available from airband radio companies or the specialist cable suppliers. These cables are compatible with the standard fittings used on most scanners and specialist suppliers will usually fit the appropriate type of connector at one end ready for use.

Care must be taken to prevent interference when routing the cable from the antenna to the receiver. Positioning the antenna directly above the receiver is ideal although it may not always be practical. Placing the antenna in a roof space may give adequate results but it is usually better to fix it outside as high as possible. If fitted to a mast, a horizontal bar should be used to keep the antenna clear of other metal parts, and it should be possible to draw an imaginary circle around the elements which avoids any other parts of the building, such as chimney stacks, fascias and so on.

Connections

Most modern receivers have antenna connections which are likely to be one of two types, known as PL259 or BNC. In recent years the BNC connection has become more popular; it is compact, easy to connect and efficient. The PL259 is heavy and more cumbersome, although equally effective. Both types can be obtained in solderless versions, making them easy to fit. Whichever type is fitted to your receiver, there are adaptors which convert BNC to PL259 and vice versa so there should be no problem with either fitting.

Some receivers, particularly in the low price range, may have one of several other kinds of antenna connection, but these are relatively unusual and it can be assumed that the majority of popular sets will be fitted with BNC or PL259 connections. Low priced receivers are probably fitted with simple extending aerials, often fixed to the receiver so that it is not possible to fit external antennas directly to the receiver. If it is intended to connect a separate aerial the simplest method is to fully close the receiver's aerial and connect the external antenna to it by means of a small crocodile clip fed from the centre core of the co-axial cable.

Antenna Manufacturers

Many of the antennas on sale today are not designed specifically for the airband listeners market. The antennas are suitable for wide coverage, not only for VHF and UHF aeronautical messages, but also for other kinds of transmissions; therefore the quality of reception is the result of a compromise in design. Wideband designs are not usually as efficient for airband listening as those specifically designed for the purpose. If your main interest is airband, then certainly try a simple home-made approach first; if this does not work by all means experiment with more sophisticated commercial systems in an attempt to improve matters, but do not be surprised if the results do not come up to expectations.

Summary

Whether you decide to choose a separate antenna to improve your listening pleasure or alternatively simply stay with the aerial provided with the receiver is a matter of choice. Many factors will influence your decision, the most important being related to the proximity of the various transmitting stations in your area. If you do most of your listening near large busy airfields or close to en route transmitter sites, the simple antenna system might well be sufficient for good quality listening. However, many of us are not in such a fortunate position. Even so, there is little doubt that an external antenna will improve the range of messages received.

However, bear in mind that many handheld scanners can be overloaded by strong signals received through an external antenna. Base station sets are designed to operate with high gain aerials and there should be little difficulty in obtaining reasonable results. An external antenna may produce disappointing results if it is connected to a lightweight handheld receiver, as the internal components are often not designed to cater for the strong signals received through an external antenna. If in doubt, refer to the manufacturer's instruction manual or speak to your supplier first.

7. High Frequency Radio

The eastern half of the North Atlantic is the responsibility of the UK National Air Traffic Services, one of a group known as 'NARTEL' – the North Atlantic Radio Telephony Network, which covers the Atlantic regions of Shanwick, Gander, Santa Maria, New York and Iceland. Shanwick handled an average of 1,150 flights each day in 2008, an increase of 1.4 per cent over 2007. However, the world wide economic recession saw a decrease in traffic at the end of 2008 and into 2009.

A high frequency radio station, Ballygirreen, near Shannon, in Ireland, relays many of the voice messages between Shanwick and the traffic over the Atlantic. Controllers at Shanwick do not have direct voice contact with pilots. A significant number of messages are also transmitted using Controller/Pilot Data Link Communications (CPDLC). Ballygirreen was originally set up to transmit messages in Morse code to the flying boats operating out of nearby Foynes, in the Shannon estuary. The callsign Shanwick is a combination of the two locations, Shannon and Prestwick.

All Atlantic flights are required to file a flight plan which will include the proposed route across land areas, together with the point of entry into the oceanic region and the proposed oceanic 'track', together with the aircraft's requested flight level, speed and time of entry into oceanic airspace. Most westbound flights from all over Europe and beyond pass through UK airspace, heading towards the North Atlantic. As they approach the 'entry points' for the Atlantic, the crew will be instructed to make contact with the Shanwick Oceanic Control Centre on the appropriate HF frequency, which in fact will be done via the radio station at Ballygirreen. The entry points are named positions on the boundaries between the Atlantic and Scottish or Irish airspace.

After the initial contact, position reports are made to Shanwick at each ten degrees of longitude, equal approximately to one hour's flying time. The report includes the aircraft's

Virgin B747-4Q8 (G-VBIG) departing London Heathrow runway 27 left
Shaun Grist

position, the time, its speed, flight level, an estimated time for reaching the next reporting point, and the next waypoint after that. Two HF frequencies are allocated to each flight, known as primary and secondary, and these vary according to the time of day and the current conditions which affect the quality of reception. The transmissions will be heard not only at Ballygirreen, but also at the other North Atlantic stations at Gander, Iceland, Santa Maria and New York.

The details included in the position reports are automatically converted into a virtual radar display at Shanwick, and the software cross checks the information with the other flights and with the original flight plan details, and alerts the controllers if it appears that a conflict is developing. None of the flights can be seen on radar, so separation of aircraft at the same level is based on time intervals and depends on the accuracy of the reports given by pilots.

High Frequency Radio

VHF and UHF aeronautical radio were discussed earlier, and both of these are very effective when the transmitter and the receiver are fairly close to each other – up to two hundred miles or so. The line-of-sight principle applies to all aircraft communications on VHF or UHF, and as these give good quality and reliable reception they are used in areas where the provision of ground stations is straightforward. However, when flights are crossing large uninhabited parts of the world, or the oceans, the use of VHF and UHF is not practical.

Instead, High Frequency (HF or Short Wave) radio is used as it is capable of operating over very long distances. It is the only accepted method at the present time of maintaining contact with flights which are flying in remote areas, although datalink communications are becoming increasingly popular and are now used for position reporting by roughly 60 per cent of trans-Atlantic flights. High Frequency transmissions for aeronautical use take place between 2 MHz and 23 MHz, in certain specific groups. Each group of frequencies is referred to as a 'family'. The frequencies in use are detailed in the appendices.

Propagation

High Frequency transmissions are able to travel across long distances because the signal from the transmitter travels upwards at an angle and is then reflected back down again. This wave of reflections can occasionally result in signals 'bouncing' around the world, although to achieve acceptable results the receiver and associated antenna system would have to be of a high standard. The atmospheric conditions which exist at the time of the transmission are known as propagation, and they can have a dramatic effect on the quality of reception. There is no reliable method for predicting how good or how bad the performance will be at any particular time. This is why the HF bands of frequencies are widely separated, so that changing from one part of the spectrum to another ensures the optimum result. Even so, quality can often be disappointing and unpredictable.

The Family System

In the North Atlantic area, six 'families' of frequencies are in use (NAT-A to NAT-F) spread across the entire range between 2 and 23 MHz.The designated frequencies are in the ranges 2, 5, 8, 11 and 17 MHz, enabling the operator to choose a frequency in each group in order to obtain the best quality. As a general rule, frequencies at the lower end of the scale will be found to be more efficient during periods when both the transmitter and the receiver are in darkness, while frequencies at the high end of the range will usually be best when both receiving and transmitting stations are in full daylight. Pilots will be allocated different frequencies as the conditions change throughout the flight.

Forecasts of the likely propagation for HF transmissions are published by the aviation authorities and in radio magazines covering the various times of the year and the hours of daylight and darkness. The frequency which has been found by experience to give the best results, in terms of volume and clarity, will be referred to as the 'primary' frequency, with a second backup frequency, in another part of the range, known as the 'secondary'

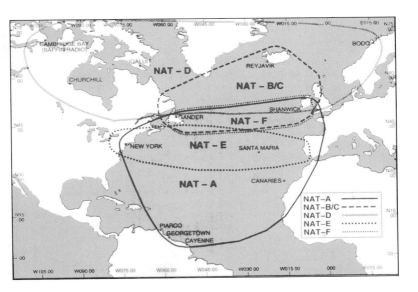

frequency. It is quite possible that as a flight proceeds across the Atlantic, the primary and secondary frequencies will be reversed as conditions change.

The allocation of frequencies varies according to the place of registration of the aircraft, partly on its route, and partly on the time of day, so that picking the correct one can be difficult for first-time listeners. However, experienced listeners to HF radio are able to predict which of the frequencies to listen to at any particular time. This, unfortunately, is one of the problems with HF radio. The fact that so many frequencies are available means that the possibility of hearing traffic on any particular one is lower than with VHF or UHF. To add to the problem, interference on HF radio is quite common, sometimes spoiling reception to such an extent that the messages are unreadable.

Advantages of HF listening

In many areas of the UK, hearing transmissions on VHF or UHF is not very successful. It is likely that the only messages that can be picked up will be from high-level

High Frequency Radio Coverage, North Atlantic, indicating the 'Family' areas
Reproduced by kind permission of the OC No.1 AIDU

flights which are almost overhead, so the satisfaction level for the enthusiast will be disappointing. However, HF radio works in a different way so the situation is completely different: the ability to receive messages between aircraft and the radio operators is not affected by the location. Although the basic HF receivers are more expensive than airband scanners, transmissions from radio operators at Ballygirreen, Santa Maria, New York and Gander are still possible.

As well as the standard position reports, including requests from pilots for clearances to climb, descend, follow a particular route or change speed, other frequently heard messages are between pilots and their bases ('company' messages) often via agency stations which pass on details or alternatively connect the pilots with their company via the telephone network – a procedure known as patching.

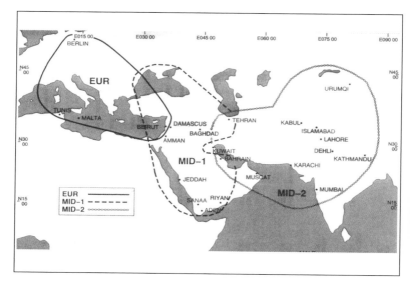

(Above) **High Frequency Radio Coverage, Europe and the Middle East**
Reproduced by kind permission of the OC No.1 AIDU

(Below) **High Frequency Radio Coverage, Africa**
Reproduced by kind permission of the OC No.1 AIDU

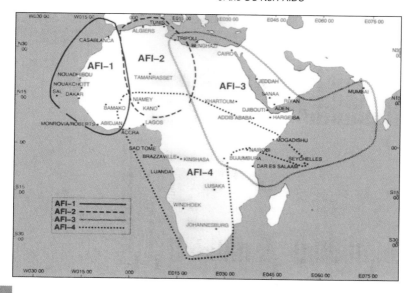

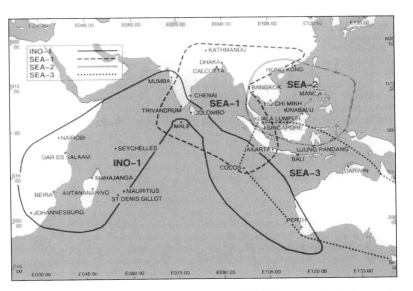

(Above) **High Frequency Radio Coverage, Indian Ocean and South East Asia**
Reproduced by kind permission of the OC No.1 AIDU

(Below) **High Frequency Radio Coverage, South Atlantic and the Caribbean**
Reproduced by kind permission of the OC No.1 AIDU

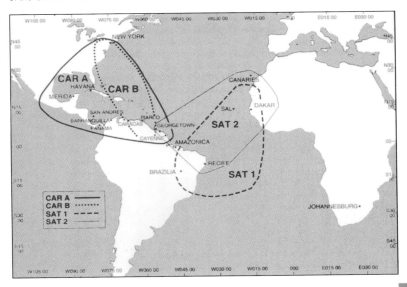

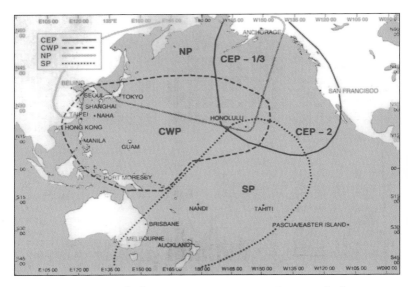

(Above) **High Frequency Radio Coverage, Pacific Ocean**
Reproduced by kind permission of the OC No.1 AIDU

(Below) **High Frequency Radio Coverage, South America**
Reproduced by kind permission of the OC No.1 AIDU

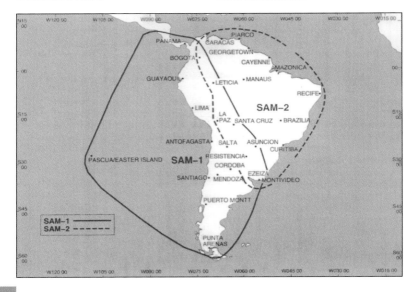

HF Radio Receivers

As well as aeronautical communications, HF radio covers hundreds of worldwide stations, most of which are not used for aeronautical purposes, so it can be a hobby in its own right. HF reception requires a radio receiver of a particular type, and they are more expensive than models suitable for VHF or UHF. There are a few handheld scanners that cover all three aeronautical bands but these usually give very disappointing results on HF and they do not compare with dedicated sets.

If cost is a consideration the airband listener will have to decide whether the extra expense is justified, especially bearing in mind that during the next ten years or so HF aeronautical communications are likely to diminish in favour of satellite coverage and new communications solutions. HF receivers are not designed only for airband use, so they will still be suitable for listening to other interesting transmissions if desired.

Aeronautical transmissions use a system known as Single Side Band (SSB), which is further divided into Upper Side Band and Lower Side Band. These mean that more channels can be accommodated within the same space and also that less interference occurs. For aviation, in order to resolve the transmissions correctly, the receiver has to be capable of operating on Upper Side Band. Some of the earlier receivers used a tuning system whereby initially the main frequency was selected. The precise frequency was then located by a sensitive tuning dial known as a Beat Frequency Oscillator which was used to finely tune the receiver. In fact, this is a relatively slow process and requires practice. For aeronautical purposes the transmission is often over before the receiver can be tuned accurately. Modern equipment has a digital frequency selection system which is far more reliable and easy to use.

As with VHF scanners, the HF frequencies can be stored in the receivers' memory, although many of the dedicated sets have no more than a few dozen memories. However, it is not possible to scan the stored frequencies, as with VHF, because the background noise prevents this. Modern HF receivers have a digital display of the frequency, together with a text indicating the particular station, a useful facility when scrolling through the memorised frequencies.

Short Wave Antennas

For VHF or UHF transmissions, as reception quality depends mainly on the line-of-sight between the transmitter and the receiver, the results are usually satisfactory provided this principle is followed. As long as the signal is not interrupted, good reception can be expected at ranges up to 50 miles for ground transmitters or 200 miles for aircraft at high level.

However, HF radio is a different matter, and reception is far less predictable regardless of location or the type of antenna. Often, a simple length of wire connected to the receiver will give results which are as good as any more expensive system. Even the built-in antenna provided with the set will give good results for the North Atlantic at certain times of the day or night. Also, experimenting with the position of the receiver can often produce dramatic changes in quality.

The quality of reception on HF depends so much on changing atmospheric conditions that the aerial system may not have a significant effect on the final result. However, it is perhaps worth trying some of the variations because one particular type might just work well in your circumstances. Unfortunately, no one particular type can be said to be better or worse than any other. It is very much a case of experimenting with the various options before a final decision is made, but even then it is quite possible that the simplest design could turn out to be the most efficient.

Most types of antenna suitable for use on HF are basically simple, consisting in the main of long lengths of wire stretched out in the open, in a roof space or around a room. If used out-of-doors a multi-strand pvc covered wire specially made for such use is recommended because it can stand the strain of being pulled in tension between two points over a considerable distance.

There are a number of designs for HF antennas:

Long Wire

This type of antenna is one of the simplest to install and yet still one of the most effective for HF reception. The wire (which is not the co-axial type) should be not less than 30 feet in length, stretched out horizontally, as high as possible. This would normally be between two buildings, or a building and a tree. Theoretically a 'north-south' installation should give the best results for traffic on the North Atlantic, although in practice this cannot always be achieved, and in any case it may not make much difference. Other factors such as the proximity of buildings or hills may well affect its efficiency.

The wire has to be insulated at each end, using ceramic insulators, and must be resistant to corrosion. A long length of wire of perhaps 50 feet needs a considerable load to stretch it to the horizontal position, therefore only the correct kind of wire is suitable. The end of the wire closest to the receiver should be run down to the receiver, as near to vertical as possible, and then to the external antenna socket on the receiver. If it is unavoidable to route the cable through the building, care must be taken to avoid any electrical circuits or sources of interference. Most radio equipment shops sell kits of suitable wire and the necessary components for HF wire antennas.

Dipole Antenna

This is a variation on the simple long-wire type of antenna, consisting of two separate horizontal wires, outside and as high as possible. Each wire should be at least 15 feet long, and insulated at both ends in the same way as the long wire type. The wires are connected via a suitable weatherproof box to a co-axial down lead (e.g. UR67), with the centre core being connected to one arm of the dipole and the outer braid to the outer arm. The co-axial cable is connected to the receiver with the appropriate connector plug.

In order to ensure that the two arms of the dipole are matched, the junction at the point of the break in the main wire can be made by using a 'balun', a type of transformer that balances the signal so that (in theory at least) it will be improved. Again, it may well be necessary to experiment with such systems to assess their efficiency as reception can change significantly from day to day. Variations of wire antennas and components for HF use are widely available.

Sloping Dipole Antenna

This is similar in design to the previous antenna, except that the wire is at an angle. It can be used as an alternative in confined spaces where the other types cannot be accommodated. In this design the wire is sloped at an angle so that the proportions are roughly equivalent to a 3:4:5 triangle, i.e. 30 feet/40 feet/50 feet, with the 50-foot arm being the actual antenna. To get the dimensions right it will be necessary to fit the highest end of the antenna wire to a mast on the chimney stack or to the highest point of a gable roof, approximately 30 feet above ground level. The lower end is fixed at a point which is roughly 40 feet horizontally from the highest point.

High Frequency Simple Long Wire Antenna Author

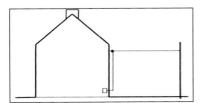

High Frequency Long Wire Dipole Antenna Author

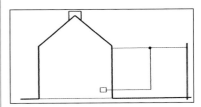

Fixing the wire at the fascia level of the average two-storey house will not usually be high enough to achieve the correct proportions. The connection to the receiver is made in the same way as for the previous dipole design, by splitting the wire at the centre and connecting a co-axial cable to the two elements.

Indoor Aerials
Often, acceptable results can be achieved by fitting a long wire antenna indoors, especially where it is not possible or convenient for an external antenna to be used. Obviously, an indoor antenna will not have to resist the weather or support its own weight. Much thinner wire can be used therefore in the roof space, around the eaves, or even under a carpet. The aim in all cases is to provide at least 30 feet of continuous wire stretched out as far as possible, although not necessarily in a straight line. If possible, two independent antennas positioned at right angles to each other will be well worth trying since each can be tried in different conditions in order to obtain the best results.

Active Antennas
This term is used to describe a type of antenna which is electrically powered, designed to match the signal at the antenna to the receiver. Active antennas are usually three or four feet in length, and are therefore suitable for fixing almost anywhere convenient. They are powered either by a mains transformer or by batteries, and although it may not be particularly better than a long wire design, it should give adequate results and is ideal where space is

High Frequency Long Wire
Dipole Antenna Author

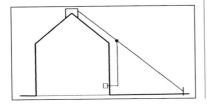

a problem or where a quick and simple system is desired. Unfortunately, the degree of success with an active antenna, as with all other types, is difficult to judge, and they can be expensive with no guarantee of satisfaction.

Earthing
It is important that any HF aerial system should be isolated from the receiver to prevent damage in the event of a lightning strike. It is also recommended that a separate earth be taken from the set to a length of copper tube or rod driven into the soil. Apart from protecting the receiver from damage, it might improve reception slightly. The necessary equipment can be purchased from radio equipment suppliers and fitted in accordance with the manufacturer's recommendations. Alternatively, if it is not earthed, make sure that the antenna is disconnected when the receiver is not being used, and never use it when there is possibility of lightning.

Aerial Tuning Units (ATUs)
One method of improving reception is possible with the use of an aerial tuning unit. They adjust the signal on any particular frequency to match the length of the antenna wire so that the best results are obtained. Adjusting the ATU improves the quality of reception as the background interference is reduced.

Conclusion
Listening to aircraft transmissions on HF is variable, to say the least. Quality and range change frequently, often in just a few hours. Sometimes the simplest of aerials, perhaps the in-built telescopic type, can give very good results; at other times reception is poor and disappointing despite the most expensive and elaborate system. Good quality receivers are expensive and for many the cost is simply not justified, especially bearing in mind that the use of HF for aeronautical transmissions is reducing with the advent of datalink for many routine messages.

8. Vitual Radar Systems

Virtual radar displays provide the airband listener and aviation enthusiast with a new tool for monitoring and tracking aircraft in real time, almost mimicking the displays seen by air traffic controllers, by taking advantage of the developments in electronic reporting systems which are now becoming standard throughout the world.

Currently, only a couple of manufacturers offer this equipment, each with its own features, so prospective purchasers will need to compare the two systems so as to ensure the most appropriate one is chosen.

The basic principles of the equipment are the same as those used by air traffic monitoring systems, which no longer rely entirely on radar, being extremely useful in those regions of the world where the ATC infrastructure for radar receiving stations is either not possible or is prohibitively expensive.

The equipment monitors the broadcast information about the progress of each flight, which is automatically broadcast at pre-determined intervals (usually every second) either through VHF receiving stations or via satellites, picked up by a short antenna and then processed by the software before being displayed on a desktop computer or laptop. The functions of the 'radar' picture can be pre-selected by the user in a variety of modes according to individual needs.

Two methods of communication are in common use by air traffic control authorities, Mode S (or Selective) and ADS-B (Automatic Dependent Surveillance – Broadcast).

Mode S allows the secondary ATC radar system to selectively interrogate the

Central England and Wales screen shot
Image generated by AirNav Systems
RadarBox – www.airnavsystems.com

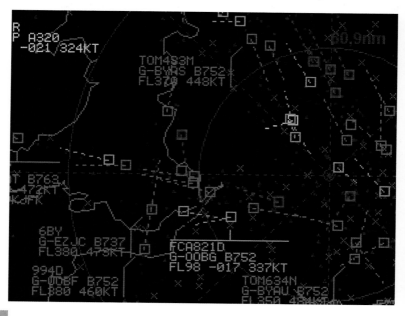

transponder on board the aircraft, using a unique 24-bit address, downloading information from the flight management system concerning the flight's identity, position, level, heading and speed, together with its rate of climb or desceny.

ADS-B automatically transmits flight information independently of any interrogation by ground-based radar systems, using the Global Positioning System, and the details of those within range are displayed on the computer screen both as a radar picture and as a list.

Where the aircraft only appear with their Mode S codes, they can oftern be identified by logging on to the Gatwick Aviation Society' website and checking its database at www.gatwickaviationsociety.org.uk

For the user, the equipment is very compact, easy to understand and set up, and reports from aircraft appear on the computer screen almost immediately. ADS-B signals are received directly from aircraft, transmitting on 1030MHz and 1090MHz, via the antenna which works on the same line-of-sight principle as VHF radio.

As with airband radio messages, if the signals are blocked by high ground or heavy buildings the information will be lost, but in good locations the range can be as much as 250 to 300 miles.

Several features can be selected by the user, depending on individual needs, and these can be stored for future use. It is also possible to record and play back any number of sessions.

The radar picture and the aircraft lists can be enlarged or reduced at will, and extra details added to the lists if required. Flights which appear on the lists can be stored and retrieved, sorted and managed in a variety of ways, producing reports and statistics chosen by the user.

The radar picture can be recorded and played back later, a useful facility if the user is not present, although a five-minute delay

Air Nav Radar Box display of the UK and north west Europe
Image generated by AirNav Systems
RadarBox – www.airnavsystems.com

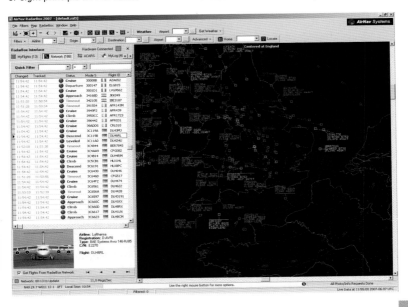

(Left) **Air Nav Radar Box display over south east England**

(Below) **Air Nav radar Box screen shot**

(Bottom) **Air Nav Radar Box screen shot showing the aircraft lists**

Images generated by AirNav Systems RadarBox – www.airnavsystems.com

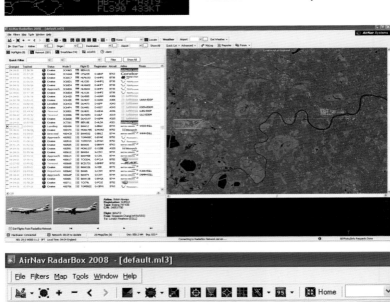

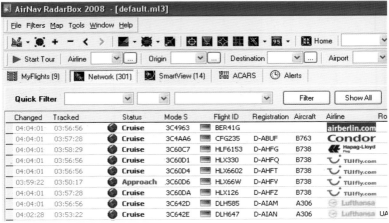

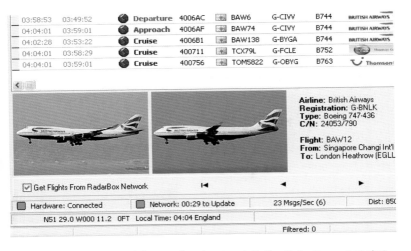

03:58:53	03:49:52	Departure	4006AC	BAW6	G-CIVV	B744	BRITISH AIRWAYS
04:04:01	03:59:01	Approach	4006AF	BAW74	G-CIVY	B744	BRITISH AIRWAYS
04:02:28	03:53:22	Cruise	4006B1	BAW138	G-BYGA	B744	BRITISH AIRWAYS
04:04:01	03:58:29	Cruise	400711	TCX79L	G-FCLE	B752	Thomson C
04:04:01	03:59:01	Cruise	400756	TOM5822	G-OBYG	B763	Thomson

Airline: British Airways
Registration: G-BNLK
Type: Boeing 747-436
C/N: 24053/790

Flight: BAW12
From: Singapore Changi Int'l
To: London Heathrow (EGLL

☑ Get Flights From RadarBox Network

| Hardware: Connected | Network: 00:29 to Update | 23 Msgs/Sec (6) | Dist: 850 |

N51 29.0 W000 11.2 0FT Local Time: 04:04 England

Filtered: 0

between the actual flights and the recording is pre-set as a security feature.

One supplier (AirNav Radar Box) offers the facility of sharing information via the Internet as part of the standard package, allowing the user to easily and automatically select any location across the world and 'see'

(Above) **Air Nav Radar Box screen shot showing details for a British Airways Boeing 747**

(Below) **Air Nav Radar Box screen shot**
Images generated by AirNav Systems RadarBox – www.airnavsystems.com

the flights in that area. With this feature, departure airports and destinations for most tracked aircraft are displayed on screen provided, of course, the details are stored in the database.

This facility is free for users in the first 12 months, after which there is a fee of 5 Euros per month. All other functions will remain unchanged.

The other system (Kinetic's SBS system) can also access information over the Internet although initial reports from users seem to indicate difficulties in downloading and applying the programs.

The latest Kinetic SBS kit (named SBS-1er), launched in the summer of 2009, also includes built-in FM and airband radio, controlled through the users computer. At the time of writing no reports of its performance were available.

The radar screen can be centred at any location, either by entering the latitude and longitude, or by selecting from a drop down menu of navigation beacons. For example, clicking on Pole Hill (a navigation aid in the north of England) will cause the screen to use that point as its centre, regardless of where the antenna is located.

With the Kinetic system, if entering a location by its co-ordinates, it first has to be converted to decimal places. Once entered, each location can be named and stored for future use. For example, 'Home' will automatically centre the screen on your home address, provided the co-ordinates have been correctly entered.

As an example, to convert 51 degrees 35 minutes 32 seconds North and 3 degrees 00 minutes 50 seconds West to decimals, the procedure is as follows:

51.35.32

Divide 32 by 60, equals .533

Add to 35, equals 35.533

Divide 35.533 by 60, equals .5922

Add to 51, equals 51.5922 North

3.00.50

Divide 50 by 60, equals .833

Add to 00, equals 00.833

Divide 00.833 by 60, equals .01388
Add to 3, equals 3.01388

All westerlies are negative values, therefore this is −3.01388 West

With the AirNav Radar Box, the process appears simpler, as merely entering a UK postcode automatically centres the radar picture on that point.

The range can also be selected, either by choosing from a list of nautical miles, or by zooming in to a close up picture. This is useful if there is a lot of traffic cluttering up the screen.

The radar labels giving flight details on AirNav Radar Box are designed so that they do not overlap, changing position as required providing the clearest display.

Air Nav Radar Box and Antenna
Image generated by AirNav Systems
RadarBox – www.airnavsystems.com

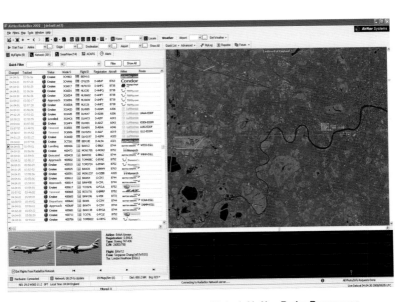

(Above) **Air Nav Radar Box screen shot over Heathrow**
Image generated by AirNav Systems
RadarBox – www.airnavsystems.com

(Below) **Air Nav Radar Box screen shot over Heathrow**
Image generated by AirNav Systems
RadarBox – www.airnavsystems.com

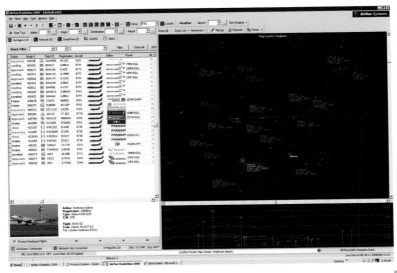

Aircraft Details

ng:	**Status:** Okay	**Squawk:**
t: 52.019°	**Altitude:** 29,850 ft	**Speed:** 466.7 kts
ng: -1.449°	**Vert. Rate:** 960	**Track:** 158.8°

Callsign : BMI3545	**Mode-S :** 4009EE	**Registration :** G-TOYB
ICAO : B733	**Type :** Boeing 737-3Q8	**Serial No :** 26311
Manufacturer :	**Operator :** BMI Baby	**Country :** United Kingdom

The contrails of each flight being tracked can be shown if required, and range rings can be added to show the distances from the centre point, plus the bearing and distance to any chosen point.

Colour is used to indicate the attitude of each aircraft (climbing, descending or level) and the data block shows the flight number, flight level, and speed in knots.

If the unit is being used near an airport, the aircraft can be tracked onto its approach, then along the runway and taxiways (at zero feet, of course) and finally into its parking bay.

With an airband scanner, it is possible to

Extract from a Kinetic sbs display showing BMI Baby aircraft details
Martin Lynch and Sons

hear the radio transmissions at the same time as seeing the aircraft on the screen, although in many cases the callsign used on the radio is not the same as the flight number.

Kinetic sbs extract showing BA 767 information
Martin Lynch and Sons

Callsign : BAW780F	**Mode-S :** 40054F	**Registration :** G-BNWX
ICAO : B763	**Type :** Boeing 767-336	**Serial No :** 25832
Manufacturer :	**Operator :** British Airways	**Country :** United Kingdom

Kintetic SBS Virtual Radar
Martin Lynch and Sons

The units are completely portable and can be taken to airports or on holiday, and require no electrical supply as they take their power from the laptop.

Kinetic sbs display over south east England
Martin Lynch and Sons

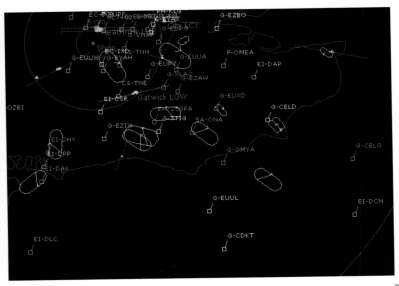

Status	Flag	Operator	Code	Callsign	Reg	ICAO	Country	Altitude	Latitude	Longitude	Speed	Track	Vert Rate	Squawk	Last Update
✧	🏴		400E72		G-BRUI	PA44	United Kingdom	0 ft	0.000°	0.000°	0.0 kts	0.0°	0		16:55:07
✧	▬	KLM	48418C		PH-BXR	B739	Netherlands	0 ft	0.000°	0.000°	0.0 kts	0.0°	0		16:55:05
●	▪	Spanair	343184		EC-KPX	A320	Spain	FL370	0.000°	0.000°	418.8 kts	223.1°	0		16:55:08
●	🏴	easyJet	400D91		G-EZAG	A319	United Kingdom	FL340	0.000°	0.000°	0.0 kts	0.0°	0		16:54:57
✈	🏴	easyJet	400F00	EZY3340	G-EZBF	A319	United Kingdom	FL380	48.650°	-0.916°	434.9 kts	352.3°	0	5535	16:55:07
✧	▮	AerArann	4CA6AB		EI-REO	AT72	Ireland	FL30	0.000°	0.000°	0.0 kts	0.0°	0		16:55:06
✈	🏴	easyJet	400AA3		G-EZEK	A319	United Kingdom	FL329	53.386°	-2.677°	523.1 kts	168.2°	0		16:54:51
✧	🏴		402AF3		G-BOJS	C172	United Kingdom	FL22	0.000°	0.000°	0.0 kts	0.0°	0		16:55:07
●	▮	RYANAIR	4CA4F7	RYR4DC	EI-DPT	B738	Ireland	0 ft	0.000°	0.000°	0.0 kts	0.0°	0		16:53:53
✈	▪		34314A	FUA1405			Spain	FL340	50.023°	2.284°	433.1 kts	128	5345		16:55:07
●	🏴	BRITISH AIRWAYS	4009F1		G-EUPW	A319	United Kingdom	FL152	0.000°	0.000°	0.0 kts	0.0°	0		16:53:33
✈	🏴	Monarch	40042C	MON660	G-MONR	A306	United Kingdom	FL340	49.310°	-1.572°	416.2 kts	355.6°	0	1063	16:55:08
✈	🏴	Monarch	401374	MON660	G-OZBR	A321	United Kingdom	FL284	51.664°	-2.878°	501.5 kts	188.5°	512		16:55:08
✈	🏴	easyJet	40094F		G-EZJJ	B737	United Kingdom	0 ft	0.000°	0.000°	431.6 kts	357.1°	0		16:53:33
✈	▮	РОССИЯ	4CA6AF		EI-DZR	A320	Ireland	FL369	49.741°	3.230°	423.9 kts	230.3°	0	3527	16:54:13
✈	🇵🇹	TP	495288	TAP614	CS-TTH	A319	Portugal	FL340	48.844°	1.035°	456.6 kts	39.8°	0		16:54:47

(Above and below)
Extracts from a Kinetic sbs screen shot list
Martin Lynch and Sons

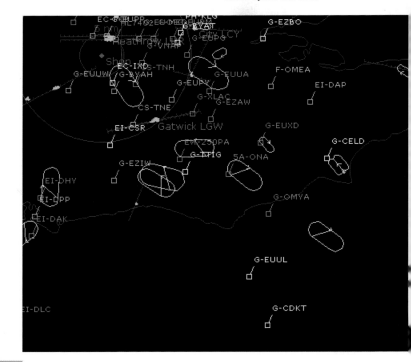

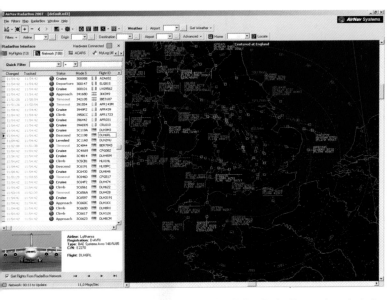

Air Nav Radar Box screen shot over the UK
Image generated by AirNav Systems RadarBox – www.airnavsystems.com

Air Nav Radar Box and Antenna
Image generated by AirNav Systems RadarBox – www.airnavsystems.com

The AirNav Radar Box package includes addition of airways, controlled airspace, airports, final approach tracks and so on as a complete package, and for the Kinetic SBS system these can be accessed through other separate websites.

In conclusion, Virtual Radar is a new exciting development in the world of aircraft tracking and identification, and revised features and updates are frequently added. The detail contained in this chapter is, therefore, subject to change although every effort has been made to maintain its accuracy, (as at summer 2009) the reader is advised to check with the suppliers and with other sources of information.

www.airnavsystems.com
www.kinetic-avionics.co.uk

Another useful site is at the Radar Spotters Forum (http://radarspotters.eu)

This provides help and advice from users and also technical information from the manufacturers.

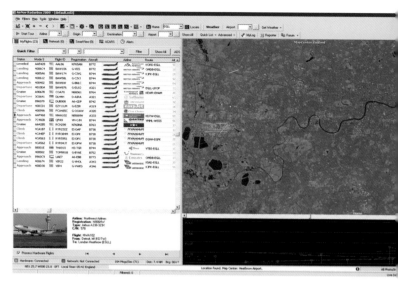

Air Nav Radar Box display of the
UK and north west Europe
Image generated by AirNav Systems
RadarBox – www.airnavsystems.com

Air Nav Radar Box screen
shot over London
Image generated by AirNav Systems
RadarBox – www.airnavsystems.com

Air Nav Radar Box screen shot
over London showing aircraft
on finals to Heathrow
Image generated by AirNav Systems
RadarBox – www.airnavsystems.com

9. Towards Better Listening

With experience and practice, the quality and quantity of airband messages can be improved through the use of additional items of equipment, or by simply understanding how the system operates. In this section, some of the factors affecting quality are examined.

Band Boxing

This term refers to the use of several transmitters and two or more VHF radio frequencies being used by one controller. This invariably happens at quiet times of the day, mostly at night, when the need for a full complement of controllers is not always necessary. Two or more sectors may be joined together into one unit, although the normal sector frequencies will still be operating. The airband listener will hear the controller talking to aircraft in both sectors, using two separate frequencies, but the pilot will only receive messages on the frequency to which his radio is tuned.

A transmission from the pilot will be received by the nearest transmitter, which will then re-broadcast it, sometimes on a different frequency, giving the listener the impression that the reception from a distant aircraft is actually much better than normal. This rebroadcasting can sometimes occur across several sectors, with (on rare occasions), transmissions being heard from aircraft a few hundred miles away. These situations almost always occur at times of the day when traffic levels are low and controller workload reduced; usually this is very early in the morning or late in the evening.

The new ATC Tower at London Heathrow
Courtesy of National Air Traffic Services

Qantas A380-841 (VH-OQA) departing London Heathrow runway 27 left
Shaun Grist

As the traffic starts to build up, the normal sector system has to be brought back into use, and the controller can be heard transferring flights to a colleague's frequency by the phrase 'recall me on frequency XXX'. Once all the aircraft in that sector have been transferred to the appropriate frequency the new controller takes over. In these cases, the controller and the pilots can be heard simultaneously on both the sector frequencies, and this can be confirmed with two receivers tuned to the two sector frequencies - identical transmissions will be heard from aircraft on the two sets at the same time. However, this does not happen very often so it may only occur occasionally in some areas.

This situation may continue for some time, until all aircraft in the various sectors have been transferred onto one single frequency. Aircraft messages being re-transmitted in this way can mean a dramatic improvement in the range of reception. An aircraft perhaps 250 miles away can have messages relayed through a receiving station possibly only 50 miles away. The re-transmitted message is then heard at full strength from a much closer location, giving the impression of very long range reception. In fact, on rare occasions, controllers and pilots can both be heard when the aircraft is more than 500 miles away from the listener, through the relay of messages over several transmitters.

Offset VHF Frequencies

Many transmissions to high-level flights are made on frequencies which are slightly higher or lower than those published or spoken by controllers. These are known as 'offsets', and the variation is as much as plus or minus 7.5 kHz.

This is because in order to obtain maximum range the ground transmissions for en route traffic are made simultaneously from two, three or four separate transmitters, and to avoid interference between the transmitters the actual frequencies used are slightly higher or lower than those published.

These offsets operate as follows:

Two transmitters in use:
Offsets are plus 2.5kHz and minus 2.5kHz.

Three transmitters in use:
Offsets are plus 5.0kHz and minus 5.0kHz, and also the published frequency.

Four transmitters in use:
Offsets are plus 2.5kHz and plus 7.5kHz, and minus 2.5kHz and minus 7.5kHz.

can be seen that the spacing between adjacent frequencies in all cases is 5kHz, because under the 25kHz system, aircraft receivers are designed to cope with these variations. However, with the 8.33kHz system, it is not technically possible to use the offset method, so at present these are only transmitted from one site. Most modern airband scanners are provided with the facility for selecting a variety of frequency steps, some as small as 0.1 kHz. A minimum of 5kHz spacing is quite common, but some older sets cannot be tuned lower than 10 or even 25kHz.

The offset system is especially useful for the airband listener, especially on the fringes of radio range. The fact that the transmission is taking place on a slightly different frequency can result in the loss of the signal altogether; airband listeners are often in locations where controllers' transmissions are difficult or impossible to receive. If the receiver is tuned to the published frequency this may in fact mean that the receiver is unable to pick up the controllers' messages at all.

So, having an airband scanner with the facility of selecting small frequency steps can be a distinct advantage in these circumstances. It is often the case that one of these offset frequencies will give better results. Tuning above or below the published frequency by small increments can often improve reception significantly, even to the point of being able to hear a controller.

How the weather affects reception

Occasionally, usually in the early morning periods in spring or autumn, the weather conditions will be such that VHF and UHF reception will be exceptional, both in range and quality. These occur only occasionally, perhaps half a dozen times a year, but it is well worth taking advantage when they do. The most common weather conditions creating improved reception is where there is a combination of fog and high pressure covering the country, which is most likely to be during the early morning and lasting perhaps until lunchtime.

Reception of controllers' messages from transmitters perhaps 200 miles away may be received without difficulty, plus other transmissions which are not usually heard, for example, continental controllers, Volmet, oceanic track clearances and even controllers in airport towers over 100 miles away. Generally a weather forecast of widespread fog during the spring or autumn will indicate that ATC transmissions will be dramatically improved.

As the fog lifts, and the weather gradually improves, the rarely heard transmissions will slowly diminish in quality, with the background noise increasing until eventually the signal will be lost altogether.

Qatar Airways A340-642/HGW (A7-AGC) late evening arrival at London Heathrow runway 27 left Shaun Grist

<table>
<tr><td colspan="5">LIFFY / BAGSO</td></tr>
<tr><td>LIFFY
2057</td><td>210</td><td>EIN208
SHAMROCK
M A320   T460</td><td>EIDW   EGCC
L975</td><td></td></tr>
<tr><td>LIFFY
2100 ↓</td><td>250</td><td>EIN192
SHAMROCK
M A321</td><td>EIDW   EGLL
UL975 UL10</td><td>310</td></tr>
<tr><td>BAGSO
2103 ↓</td><td>290
200</td><td>EIN357
SHAMROCK
M A320   300</td><td>EDDM   EIDW
UL26 UL70 UV14</td><td>SOPAX
2057
200</td></tr>
<tr><td>BAGSO
2104 ↓</td><td>290
240</td><td>EIN611
SHAMROCK
M A320</td><td>EHAM   EIDW
UL26 UL70 UV14</td><td>SOPAX
2059
340
200</td></tr>
<tr><td>BAGSO
2157 ↑</td><td>180
160</td><td>RYR449L
RYANAIR
M B738</td><td>EGGP   EIDW
L10 L70 V14</td><td>PENIL
2147
180
180</td></tr>
<tr><td>T-IOM</td><td colspan="2">Find</td><td>Copy</td><td>Send to</td></tr>
</table>

Part of an Electronic Flight Progress Strip display. These are gradually replacing the use of traditional paper strips throughout the UK
Courtesy of National Air Traffic Services

Attenuators

The dictionary definition of 'attenuate' is to 'reduce in force or value', and this is the function of an attenuator fitted between the antenna and the receiver. The signal reaching the set is reduced in strength, the degree varying according to the value of the attenuator. A number of models have built-in attenuators, usually in the range of 10 or 20 decibels, which is brought into the circuit using a button or slide switch on the receiver. This reduces the signal strength, so if part of the transmission is weak it will probably be eliminated entirely when the attenuator is used.

If reception is loud and clear, there is no need to bother with an attenuator as they are normally used to cancel out unwanted signals. There are often occasions when the quality of reception is spoiled by interference or some other 'breakthrough' transmission which manages to interrupt the original message at a critical point. In these cases, the use of one or more attenuators is particularly useful, and with some trial and error it is usually possible to improve the quality of reception.

For more flexibility, and for those receivers that do not contain a built-in attenuator, it is possible to purchase individual attenuators for different values, which can be fitted either singly or in combination so as to produce different degrees of attenuation.

Attenuators of this type are plugged directly into the aerial socket on the receiver either singly or in multiples, to give the required level of reduction, and the aerial feed is then connected to the attenuator. The attenuators can be used in any combination. If a 3 db and two 6db attenuators are purchased, it is possible to use them in varying selections to give attenuations of 3, 6, 9, 12 and 15 decibels – usually more than enough for most situations.

Attenuators are normally supplied with BNC connections as standard, being appropriate for use with the majority of VHF/UHF scanners. Operating a hand-held scanner with an external aerial can sometimes cause problems with reception quality so using attenuators in these situations can be a positive advantage.

Amplifiers

In areas of poor reception on UHF or VHF, possibly because of location or distance from a transmitter, the quality can often be improved by using a separate amplifier which is placed between the antenna and the receiver (usually close to the receiver). Amplifiers are powered either from the mains or from a battery. Unfortunately, in common with other so called improvements, they may not always be beneficial. In some cases, they actually have the opposite effect and produce results which are far worse than those experienced without amplification. Some models are specifically designed for VHF airband use, and these have been proved to be most effective. However, disappointing results cannot be ruled out. Your supplier may be persuaded to agree to a refund or exchange if the unit does not produce an acceptable improvement.

Amplifiers increase the intensity of the signal received via the antenna, but at the same time they may increase interference to an unacceptable degree, even to the point where maximising the squelch has no effect. In other areas, messages which are not normally heard may be received with very reasonable results. Surprisingly, it is possible that reception quality can be improved by the use of an amplifier in conjunction with attenuators, trying various combinations to give the best result. The same general rule applies to amplifiers as with other equipment, that is, the most costly may not give the best performance.

Tape Recording

There are definite benefits in recording aeronautical transmissions, especially through a voice activated recorder. For the newcomer in particular, understanding the language and the structure of messages requires a degree of experience so being able to replay them means they can be analysed and replayed as often as required. Newcomers to airband listening will find the rapid and often clipped speech used by controllers and pilots very difficult to follow. Add to this the wide use of standard phrases and acronyms and the problem becomes even greater, so the beginner should benefit by being able to listen to recorded messages.

Another benefit is ability to record information when the listener is not present – for example, overnight, or when the actual transmissions are few and far between, as with the emergency services. With a voice-activated machine, the tape only runs when sounds are detected so nothing is wasted. The tape can be checked later for any messages and it will then be possible to listen to all the messages with virtually no break between them.

However, one problem with airband involves tape recorder connection. Many are provided with outlets for extension speakers or earphones but these are grossly overpowered for use with a tape recorder, and only a few on the market have the correct type. This can easily be overcome through the use of resistors fitted to the cable connecting the receiver and the recorder as these reduce the strength of the signal to the correct level. Resistors are inexpensive, and two or three of different values can be purchased quite cheaply. The resistor is simply soldered into the centre core of the lead between the receiver and the recorder.

A typical value of a resistor is 100K. This can be tried first, but if the results are not acceptable, experiment with ones of a higher or lower value. They take only minutes to fit and are well worth the expense in terms of improved quality. Without a direct cable connection, the only alternative is to use the built in microphone but the quality of the recording will be much lower with the possibility of unwanted noise as well.

With most scanners fitted with loudspeaker connections, plugging in a tape recorder cable causes the internal speaker to be disconnected. This can be overcome quite easily by using a 'splitter' which is plugged into the outlet on the receiver. This splits the signal so that one connection can be made to the tape recorder while the other connection is made to a separate loudspeaker. This allows the listener to hear the messages as well as recording at the same time. Very good results can be obtained provided some thought is given to developing the end product and there is no doubt that many items of interest that would otherwise be missed can be captured and analysed.

Computer Control

A few scanners now have the facility for being managed through a personal computer. The receiver is connected to the PC via a special connecting lead and an interface unit. Frequencies can be entered and sorted on the computer and down-loaded to the receivers memory. Various kinds of reports can also be produced. It is doubtful if this arrangement is appropriate for the listener whose only interest is in airband since the need to manage and rearrange frequencies is relatively rare. Also, of course, access to a PC is required and the interface and software are not particularly cheap. For further details contact one of the suppliers in the appendices.

Appendix A. VHF and UHF Receivers

The following schedule covers most VHF and UHF scanners currently available, and a few also cover the HF bands. However, the HF models are unlikely to match the standard of dedicated short-wave receivers, so their performance is likely to be disappointing. If your interest is in HF, discuss your requirements with one of the suppliers given in the appendices. When considering the purchase of a scanner, bear in mind the following basic points:

A dedicated model usually performs better than a wideband model.

Almost all modern scanners have steps of 5kHz or less, **but check this point carefully** before purchase;

Many secondhand models do **not** have 5kHz steps.

In all cases, confirm the specification details with the supplier.

MODEL	HAND HELD/ BASE	FREQUENCY RANGE	MEMORIES	PRICE GUIDE	COMMENTS
ALINCO DJ-X 2000	H	VHF/UHF/HF	2000	£400	5 & 8.33 steps
ALINCO DJ-X3	H	VHF/UHF	700	£120	5 & 8.33 steps
ALINCO DJ-X7	H	VHF/UHF	1000	£145	5 & 8.33 steps
ALINCO DJ-X30	H	VHF/UHF	1000	£145	5 & 8.33 steps
AOR MINI	H	VHF/UHF	1000	£250	5 & 8.33 steps
AOR 8200 MK 3	H	VHF/UHF/HF	1000	£450	5 & 8.33 steps
AOR 8600 MK 2	B	VHF/UHF/HF	1000	£650	5 & 8.33 steps
GRE PSR 282	H	VHF/UHF	200	£85	5 & 8.33 steps
GRE PSR-295	H	VHF/UHF	1000	£120	5 & 8.33 steps

ICOM IC-RX7	H	VHF/UHF	1650	£250	5 & 8.33 steps
ICOM IC-R3E	H	VHF/UHF	450	£350	Includes 50mm TV
ICOM IC-R5E	H	VHF/UHF	1250	£200	5 & 8.33 steps
ICOM IC-R20	H	VHF/UHF/HF	1250	£450	
MAYCOM FR-100	H	VHF/UHF	150	£75	
MAYCOM AR108	H	VHF	99	£70	5 kHz steps
STEEPLETONE SAB 9 Mk III	H	VHF	None	£35	Continuous tuning
STEEPLETONE SAB 2006	H	VHF	None	£50	Continuous tuning
UNIDEN UBC 30 XLT	H	VHF	200	£65	5 & 8.33 steps
UNIDEN UBC 72XLT	H	VHF	100	£100	5 & 8.33 steps
UNIDEN UBC 92XLT	H	VHF	200	£200	
UNIDEN UBC 230XLT	H	VHF/UHF	2500	£125	
UNIDEN UBC 785XLT	B	VHF/UHF	1000	£285	5 & 8.33 steps
UNIDEN UBC 800XLT	B	VHF/UHF	6000	£285	5 & 8.33 steps
YAESU VR-5000	B	VHF/UHF/HF	2000	£550	
YAESU VR-500	H	VHF/UHF/HF	1000	£200	

Most of the airlines that operate in UK airspace are listed here, but those which use the airline name as the callsign (for example, Air France, Ryanair, Delta and so on) have been omitted. Many flights can be identified by the number following the callsign, as it often matches the timetable for the particular airline. However, many now use numbers and letters which bear no resemblance to the timetable, so a specialist publication which decodes these is essential.

CALLSIGN	OPERATOR
Abbas	Abbas Air
Abex	Airborne Express
Act	Ait Air Charter and Travel
Adria	Adria Airways
Advent	A T S / Vulcan
Aerocharter	Aero Charter Midlands Ltd
AeroCroat	AeroCroatia
Air Chester	City Air
Air Discovery	Discovery Airways
Air Force 1	USAF Carrying the President
Air Force 2	USAF Carrying the Vice President
Air Mike	Continental Micronesia
Air Nav	Air Navigation and Trading Ltd
Air Opal	Air Cote D'Opale
Air Shuttle	Mesa Airlines
Airbridge	Hunting Cargo
Airflex	Flexair Ltd
Airgoat	Airborne School of Flying
AirScan	Air Scandic
Airshot	Birmingham Aerocentre
Airtax	Birmingham Aviation
Airwork	Airwork Services Training
Alexandra	Euroair
Algarve	Avialgarve SA
Amberwell	First City Air
Amex	A R M Palfem, Spain
Amiri	Qatar Government / Royal Flight
AmTran	American Trans Air
Anglesey	R A F Valley
Apolloair	Apollo Airlines
Army Air	Army Air Corps
Ascot	Royal Air Force - Air Support Command
Asia	Japan Asia Airlines
Asian Express	Air Asia
Astel	Air Service Training Ltd
Astronaut	D L R Flugbetrieb
Atas	Air Gambia
Atlantic	Air Atlantique
Auctions	A D T Aviation Ltd
Avenger	A Haig-Thomas (Securities) Ltd
Avian	Avia Airlines
Aviatrans	M T M Aviation
Avcon	Execujet Charter
Avro	British Aerospace, Woodford
Ayline	Aurigny Air Services
Aztec Air	Air Bristol
Backer	British Charter
Bafair	Royal Belgian Air Force
Bahrain One	The Amiri Royal Flight
Batman	Ratioflug
Beeline	Biggin Hill Executive Aviation
Berne Eagle	Eagle Air Service SA
Beryl	Emerald Air
Beaupair	Aviation Beauport
Big A	Arrow Air
Biggles	Express Air Charter
Bird Dog	Crispe Aviation Services
Bizjet	Hamlin Jet Ltd
Biztravel	Business Air Travel
Blackbox	DRA, Bedford
Blackburn	British Aerospace, Scampton
Blacksea	MNG Air
Blue	USAF European Tanker TDY
Blue Eagle	Eagle Air Ltd
Blue Ridge	Atlantic Coast Airways
Blue Wings	Air Taxi Wings AG
Bluebird	Finnaviation O/Y

Blue Island	AirX
BlueJet	Skynet Airlines
Bond	Bond Helicopters
Box	Tiphook plc
Boxer	United States - ANG Bureau
Brenex	Brenair Ltd
Bristol	British Aerospace, Filton
British	British Regional Airlines
Brittany	Brit Air
Broadway	F R Aviation
Brown	USAF European Tanker TDY
Browntail	United Parcels Service
Budgetjet	Ryanair UK
Buzzard	Butane Buzzard Ltd.
Byte	Birmingham Aerocentre
Calibrator	C A A Calibration Flight
Cactus	United Airlines
Camair	Cameroon Airlines
Cambridge	Hawkair Carriers
Canadian	Canadian Airlines
Canforce	Canadian Armed Forces
Capital	Capital Radio, London - 'Eye in the Sky'
Cargosur	Cargosur
CargoTrans	Ukrainian Cargo Airlines
Catbird	United States Navy
Cathay	Cathay Pacific Airways
Cayman	Cayman Airways Ltd
Cedar Jet	Middle East Airlines
Channex	Jet2
Cheshair	Cheshire Air Training School
China	Air China
Citrus	Air Tran
City	KLM Cityhopper
CityIreland	CityJet
Clan King	Air Sinclair
Clansman	Airwork Ltd
Clifton	Bristol Flying Centre
Clog	Scholl [UK] Ltd
Cloud	Skytrek
Clue	USAF - HQ USEUCOM
Coastline	Coastair A/S
Coastrider	BASE Airlines
Compass	Compass Helicopters, Bristol
Connie	Connie Kalitta Services
Conoco	Continental Oil Inc
Consort	Consort Aviation
Contract	Air Contractors
Crane	R W L GmbH
Cutlass	Air Foyle Airways
Cygnet	British Aerospace Flying College
Dantax	Aalborg Air Taxi
Dantrans	Danish Air Transport
Dargobert	Quick Air Jet
Delta Ice	MD Icelandic Airlines
Directflight	Directflight Ltd
Dolomiti	Air Dolomiti Sri
Donex	Donaghue Aviation Air Charter
Dorada	Aeronaves La Dorada, Spain
Dove	Danube-Air
Drenair	Drenair SA
Dubai	Dubai Government
Duke	US Army - 207 AvnCoy
Dynamite	Dynamic Air BV
Dynasty	China Air Lines
Eastex	Eastern Air Executive
Eastline	Nordic European Airways
Easy	Easyjet
Echo-Victor	Evergreen International Airlines
Echojet	Berlin European
Eclipse	World Airlines
Electricity	South Western Electricity Board
Emerald	Westair
Enterprise	Air Enterprise
Envoy	FlyJet
Essex	Essex Police
Eurocat	Cat Aviation
Eurocharter	European Airlines
EuroExpress	Avanti Air
Eurofly	Eurofly Spa, Italy
Europa	Air Europa
Eurotrans	European Air Transport
Eurowings	European Wings
Evergreen	Evergreen International Airlines
Evergreen	Defence Research Agency
Exam	C A A Examiners
Exjet	Executive Jet Aviation
Expo	Excel Airways
Express	Federal Express
Falcon	Falcon Aviation AB
Fastcargo	Race Cargo Airlines
Fanum	Automobile Association
FedEx	Federal Express
Findon	Fast Helicopters
Firestone	Dravidian Air Services

Flagship	Pinnacle Airlines	Jetplan	Memrykord Ltd
Flamingo	Eurowings	JetSet	Air 2000
Flapjack	Heritage Aviation Developments	Jetwing	All Leisure Airways
Flo West	Florida West	Joker	Germania
FlyDuo	DUO Airways	Jolly	USAF - 67 ARRS
FlyStar	Astraeus	Kestrel	MY Travel Airways
Food	Foodbrokers Ltd	Kilro	Air Kilroe
Fordair	Ford Motor Co	King	USAF- 67 ARRS
Fox Club	Leicester Aero Club	Kingfisher	Kingair Flying Club
Foxtrot Alpha	French Air Force	Kitty	RAF – 32 (The Royal) Squadron
Foxtrot Papa	Aeroleasing S.A.		
Foxtrot Romeo	Swiss Air Ambulance	Kittyhawk	RAF - 32 (The Royal) Squadron
Foyle	Air Foyle		
France Cargo	EFIS Cargo	Kiwi	Royal New Zealand Air Force
Frankenair	F A I Air Services		
Freeway	Freeway Air BV	Knightway	Knight Air
Frobisher	European Airlines	Koreanair	Korean Air
Gauntlet	Quinetiq / A & A E E , Boscombe Down	Kris	Air Foyle Charters
		Lager	USAF European Tanker TDY
Gemstone	Emerald Airways		
German Link	Regionair	Lark	USAF - 55 WRS
Getaway	USA 3000 Airlines	Ledair	Leadair-Unijet SA
Gibair	G B Airways Ltd	Leisure	Leisure International
Gipsy	Interline	Lifeline	Aeromedicaire Ltd
Glace	Air Greenland	Lion Helicopters	British International
Golf November	Air Gabon	Liver	Liverpool Flying School Ltd
Granite	Business Air		
Greenbird	Skyjet	Lomas	Lomas Helicopters Ltd.
Grosvenor	Grosvenor Air Services	Lonex	London Flight Centre
Gulf	Gulf Air	Longhorn	Express One International
Hamilton	Air Nova		
Harmony	HMY Airlines	Lord	US Army - 56th AvnCoy
Hawker	British Aerospace, Dunsfold	Lynton	Lynton Aviation, Heathrow
Hamilton	Air Nova	Magodan	North East Cargo
Helibus	CHC Scotia Helicopters	Majan	Oman Air Force
Helimed	First Air	Manta	Woodford Flight Centre
Helispeed	Biggin Hill Helicopters	Maroc	Royal Air Maroc
Heritage	Jet Heritage Ltd.	Marshall	Marshall Of Cambridge Ltd
HiWay	Highland Airways		
Horizon	Horizon Air Taxi Ltd	Martin	Martin Baker Ltd
Husky	Royal Norwegian Air Force	Merlin	Rolls-Royce
		Mermaid	Air Alsie
Iceair	Icelandair	Metman	Meteorolgical Flight
Icebird	Islandsflug	Midland	British Midland Airways
India [+4 Digits]	Italian Air Force	Minair	Civil Aviation Authority [U K]
Indonesia	Garuda		
Intersun	Sunways	Mining	3M Corporation
Irish Trans	Irish Air Transport	Moonflower	Neos
Janes	Emerald Airways	Mooseline	West Air Executive
Japanair	Japan Air Lines	Moras	Air Moravia
Jet European	Jet Ltd	Nacair	Canafrica Spa
Jetlink	Express Jet Airways	Navigator	Novair

Neatax	Northern Executive Aviation
Newpin	British Aerospace, Chester
Nimbus	Nimbus Aviation
Nitro	T N T
Norland	Flugfelag Nordurlands
Normandie	Air Normandie
Norseman	Norskair
Nugget	DRA , Farnborough
Old	USAF C-130 European TDY
Omega	Aeromega
Orange	Air Holland
Oriental Air	Oriental Airlines Ltd
Oryx	Oman Aviation
Osprey	P L M Dollar Group
Ostfries	OLT GmbH
Pakistan	Pakistan International
Para	Army Parachute Centre
Pathfinder	Leeds Central Helicopters
Pengiun	British Antarctic Survey
Picair	Air Méditerranée
Pirate	Air South West
Pizaz	Pizaz European
Portugal	Air Portugal
Predator	Eagle Airways
Prospair	Prospair Air Charter
Provost	Bearing Services Ltd
Puma	Phoenix Aviation
Quality	TNT Airways
Quid	USAF European Tanker TDY
Rabbit	Rabbit-Air AG
Rafair	Royal Air Force
Rainbow	RAF - 32 [The Royal] Squadron
Ranger	Ranger Defence Products Ltd
Rapex	B A C Aircraft
Readymix	R M C Group Services
Redair	Redhill Aviation
Rega	Swiss Air Ambulance
Rhinoair	Heathrow Jet Charter
Riverside	Universal Air Transport
Roman	RM Aviation
Rosie	Rosenbalm / Emery
Rushton	Flight Refuelling Ltd.
S-Tail	SN Brussels Airlines
Saabcraft	SAAB Aircraft AB
Sabre	Sabre Airways
Saltaire	Edinburgh Air Charter
Sam	USAF - 89 AW
Sapphire	British Aerospace, Filton
Sark	Sark International Airways
Sarnair	Channel Aviation Ltd
Saudia	Saudia
Scanbird	Air-X A/S
Scandinavian	SAS
Scandy	SAS
Scanvip	Air Express A/S
Scanwings	Malmo Aviation
Schreiner	Schreiner Airways
Scillonia	Isles of Scilly Skybus
Scotair	Euroscot Airways
Scotwing	Cumbernauld Flight Centre
Seeline	Barnes Olson Aeroleasing
Seychelles	Air Seychelles
Shamrock	Aer Lingus
Shamu	USAF - 68 ARW
Sharif	Balkh Airlines
Sharjah	Sharjah Government
Shell	Shell Aviation
Short	Short Brothers
Shuttle 2	BA Shuttle Heathrow-Manchester
Shuttle 3	BA Shuttle Manchester-Heathrow
Shuttle 4	BA Shuttle Heathrow-Belfast
Shuttle 5	BA Shuttle Belfast-Heathrow
Shuttle 6	BA Shuttle Heathrow-Glasgow
Shuttle 7	BA Shuttle Glasgow-Heathrow
Shuttle 8	BA Shuttle Heathrow-Edinburgh
Shuttle 9	BA Shuttle Edinburgh-Heathrow
Simflight	Simulated Flight Training
Sky Express	Skyways AB
Skyjet	Skyjet
Skyman	Air Foyle [Executive] Ltd
Skyshare	Air Luxor / NetJets Europe
Skytruk	Trans Air Link [Miami]
Skywatch	Skywatch Ltd
Skywork	Scottish Flyers Ltd.
Snoopy	Air Traffic GmbH
Snowbird	Air Atlanta Europe
Southern Air	Southern Air Transport Inc
Sovereign	Imperial Commuter

Spar	USAF - 58 MAS
Sparrowhawk	Edinburgh Air Centre
Special	Metropolitan Police
Speedbird	British Airways
Speedcat	Cougar Air
Speedfox	Jet Air A/S
Speedway	Deutsche B A
Speedwing	Speedwings SA
Spirit	Norwegian Aviation College
Springbok	South African Airways
Stapleford	Stapleford Flying Club
Stardust	N A G [Germany]
Starline	Varmlandsflyg
Streamline	Streamline Aviation
Suckling	Suckling Airways
Sudanair	Sudan Airways
Summer Express	Venus Airlines
Sunbeam	EVEX Flug
Sunjet	Scanair
Sunscan	Sun Air / British Airways Express
Sunshine	Sunshine Aviation SA
Sunturk	Pegasus Airlines, Turkey
Sunwing	Spanair
Swallow	Air South West
Swedic	Royal Swedish Air Force
SwedeStar	City Airlines
Swiftair	Air Swift
Swiss	Swiss International Airlines
Syrianair	Syrianair
Tango-Charlie	Air Tanzania
Tango-Lima	Trans Mediterranean Airways
Tarnish	British Aerospace, Warton
Taunusair	Taunus Air
Teebird	West Freugh T & E E
Tennant	British Aerospace, Prestwick
Tester	Empire Test Pilots School
Thai Inter	Thai International
Titan	United States Marine Corps
Topcat	Helicopter Services
Topjet	Thomas Cook Airlines UK
Torair	Toros Air
Transat	Air Transat
Trent	Trent Air Services
Trout	USAF - 89 MAW
Tulipair	Tulip Air
Tunair	Tunis Air

Turkair	THY - Turkish Airlines
Tutor	G B Air Academy
Ukay	Air U K
Uni	Community Express
Universair	Universair
Upsco	United Parcel Service
Uzbek	Uzbekistan Air
Vale	Woodvale Avistion Co Ltd
Vectis	Pilatus-Britten-Norman
Venus Star	Venus Airways
Venus	USAF - 89 AW
Viasa	V I A S A
Vickers	Vickers Group plc
Victor Kilo	Airbus Industrie
Victory	Transwede Airways
Viennair	Viennair GmbH
Viking	Premiair
Vipflight	Aeroleasing
Watchdog	Ministry of Agriculture, Fisheries and Farming
Waterski	Trans States
Wayne Air	B W Air Services
Wessex	Wessex Aviation
West Indian	British West Indian Airways
Westland	Westland Helicopters
Wexford	EuroCeltic Airways
Whitbread	Whitbread Group
White Star	Star Air Denmark
White	USAF European Tanker TDY
Wigwam	C S E Aviation
Witchcraft	Flugdienst Fehlhaber GmbH
Wizard	Merlin Flying College
Woodair	Woodgate Air Services Ltd
Woodstock	Oxford Air Services
World	World Airways
Worldgate	Volkswagen AG
Wrangler	Tradewinds International Airlines
Yemini	Yemen Airways
Yeoman	Foster-Yeoman Group plc
YooBee	United Biscuits plc
Yorkair	Yorkshire Flying Services
Yugair	Air Yugoslavia / JAT
Zagal	Zagreb Airlines
Zambex	Zambia Express Airways
Zap	Titan Airways
Zebra	African Safari Airways
Zimex	Zimex Aviation

Appendix C. Airfield Directory

The following information covers most airfields and airports in the UK and Ireland. In many cases, individual frequencies may only be used on rare occasions, so do not expect to hear messages on them all.

Certain abbreviations have been used, as follows:

AFIS	Aerodrome Flight Information Service
ATIS	Automatic Terminal Information Service
CAC	Centralised Approach Control
DAAIS	Danger Area Activity Information Service
MAS	Middle Airspace Service
METRO	Pilot to Metro Voice Call
PAR	Precision Approach Radar
PMSV	Pilot to Metro Service
SRA	Surveillance Radar Approach

AIRFIELD	SERVICE	VHF	UHF
ABERDEEN/DYCE	APPROACH	119.050	
	RADAR	134.100	
		128.300	
	TOWER	118.100	
	GROUND	121.700	
	ATIS	121.850	
ABERPORTH	INFO	119.650	338.925
ALDERNEY	APPROACH	128.650	
	TOWER	125.350	
	GROUND	130.500	
BALDONNEL/CASEMENT	AREA	122.800	
	APPROACH	122.000	
	RADAR(DUBLIN)	122.300	
	TOWER	123.500	
	GROUND	123.100	
BARKSTON HEATH	APPROACH(CRANWELL)		280.775
	DEPARTURES	119.375	355.950
	DIRECTOR		282.600
	SRA	123.300	378.525
	TOWER	120.425	281.225
	GROUND		389.450
	ATIS		293.450
BELFAST/ALDERGROVE	APPROACH	128.500	278.350
	RADAR	120.900	
	TOWER	118.300	278.350
	GROUND	121.750	
	RAF OPERATIONS		264.800
	ATIS	128.200	
BELFAST CITY	APPROACH	130.850	
	RADAR	130.850	
	TOWER	122.825	

AIRFIELD	SERVICE	VHF	UHF
BELFAST CITY (continued)	ATIS	136.625	
	HANDLING	129.750	
BENBECULA	APPROACH	119.200	
	TOWER	119.200	
	ATIS	113.950	
BENSON	CAC		278.600
	APPROACH	136.450	376.650
	ZONE	120.900	
	DIRECTOR	136.450	356.125
	PAR	136.450	283.075
		123.300	277.675
	TOWER	127.15	318.100
	GROUND	121.800	
	ATIS		282.525
BIGGIN HILL	APPROACH	129.400	
	TOWER	134.800	
	ATIS	121.875	
BIRMINGHAM	APPROACH	118.050	
	RADAR	131.325	
	TOWER	118.300	
	GROUND	121.800	
	ATIS	136.025	
	DELIVERY	121.925	
BLACKBUSHE	AFIS	122.300	
	RADIO	122.300	
BLACKPOOL	APPROACH	119.950	
	RADAR	135.950	
	TOWER	118.400	
	ATIS	121.750	
BOSCOMBE DOWN	APPROACH	130.000	233.850
	RADAR		371.825
	DIRECTOR		282.675
	ZONE	126.700	256.500
	PAR	130.000	369.250
	TOWER	130.750	338.475
	GROUND	130.75	262.950
	ATIS		275.725
BOULMER	AIR/GROUND	123.100	249.625
			282.800
BOURNEMOUTH	APPROACH	119.475	
	RADAR	118.650	
	TOWER	125.600	
	GROUND	121.700	
	ATIS	133.725	

AIRFIELD	SERVICE	VHF	UHF
BRISTOL	APPROACH	125.650	
	RADAR	136.075	313.450
	TOWER	133.850	
	GROUND	121.925	
	ATIS	126.025	
BRISTOL/FILTON	APPROACH	122.725	341.325
	RADAR	124.950	341.325
	DIRECTOR	127.975	336.475
	TOWER	132.350	243.050
BRIZE NORTON	CAC	124.275	389.575
	APPROACH	127.250	297.800
			362.300
	ZONE	119.000	
	RADAR	133.750	264.775
	SRA	126.500	339.850
	TOWER	123.725	379.750
			257.800
	GROUND	121.725	396.850
	OPERATIONS	130.075	386.825
	ATIS		259.000
CAMBRIDGE	APPROACH	123.600	
	RADAR	124.975	
	TOWER	122.200	
	ATIS	134.600	
CAMPBELTOWN	AFIS	125.900	
CARDIFF	APPROACH	126.625	251.375
	RADAR	125.850	251.375
	TOWER	125.000	
	ATIS	132.475	
CARLISLE	APPROACH	123.600	
	TOWER	123.600	
	ATIS	118.425	
CHALGROVE	APPROACH(BENSON)	120.900	
	TOWER (RADIO)	125.400	
CHIVENOR	AIR/GROUND	130.200	252.800
CHURCH FENTON	APPROACH	126.500	233.450
			362.300
	DIRECTOR		338.700
	PAR	123.300	379.475
	TOWER	122.100	234.100
	GROUND	121.950	341.225
COLERNE	APPROACH	120.075	374.825
	TOWER	120.075	372.575
	ATIS		277.850

AIRFIELD	SERVICE	VHF	UHF
CONINGSBY	CAC		277.775
	APPROACH	120.800	282.725
		122.100	362.300
			376.350
	DIRECTOR		277.500
			344.0
	PAR	123.300	281.125
			341.200
	TOWER	124.675	340.250
	GROUND	122.100	279.075
	OPERATIONS		234.675
	ATIS		280.300
CONNAUGHT	TOWER	130.700	
	GROUND	121.900	
CORK	APPROACH	119.900	
	RADAR	118.800	
	TOWER	119.300	
		121.700	
	GROUND	121.850	
	ATIS	120.925	
COSFORD	APPROACH	135.875	376.425
	TOWER	128.650	378.650
	GROUND	128.650	241.400
COTTESMORE	CAC		277.775
	APPROACH		281.900
	DIRECTOR	123.300	379.075
	DEPARTURES	130.200	278.450
	ZONE	130.200	231.725
	TALKDOWN	123.300	338.250
			339.325
	TOWER	122.100	369.350
			257.800
	GROUND	122.100	308.825
	ATIS		262.625
COVENTRY	APPROACH	119.250	
	RADAR	123.825	
	TOWER	119.250	
		118.175	
	GROUND	121.700	
	ATIS	126.050	
CRANFIELD	APPROACH	122.850	
	TOWER	134.925	
		122.850	
	ATIS	121.875	
CRANWELL	MAS		277.775
	APPROACH	119.375	280.775
			362.300
	DEPARTURES	119.375	275.675
	DIRECTOR	123.300	284.325

AIRFIELD	SERVICE	VHF	UHF
CRANWELL (continued)	TALKDOWN	123.300	338.275
			378.525
	TOWER	125.050	268.625
			257.800
	GROUND		240.425
	ATIS	135.675	233.625
CULDROSE	APPROACH	134.050	378.550
	RADAR		369.225
			241.400
	DIRECTOR	123.300	313.600
	TALKDOWN	123.300	293.825
			296.675
	TOWER	122.100	297.775
	GROUND		318.100
	ATIS		231.850
DISHFORTH	APPROACH(Topcliffe)	122.100	293.775
			362.300
	TOWER	122.100	278.225
	GROUND		371.975
	OPERATIONS		242.250
DONCASTER SHEFFIELD	APPROACH	126.225	
	TOWER	128.775	
	RADAR	126.225	283.425
	ATIS	134.950	
DONEGAL	APPROACH (Shannon)	127.500	
	TOWER/GROUND	129.800	
	ATIS	129.925	
DUBLIN	APPROACH	121.100	
		119.550	
		119.925	
		118.500	
	RADAR	124.650	
		129.175	
		136.050	
		126.250	
	DIRECTOR	119.550	
		118.500	
	TOWER	118.600	
	GROUND	121.800	
	DELIVERY	121.875	
	ATIS	124.525	
DUNDEE	APPROACH/TOWER	122.900	
DUNKESWELL	AIR/GROUND	123.475	
DURHAM TEES VALLEY	APPROACH	118.850	
	RADAR	118.850	
	DIRECTOR	128.850	
	TOWER	119.800	
	ATIS	132.375	

AIRFIELD	SERVICE	VHF	UHF
DUXFORD	INFORMATION	122.075	
EAST MIDLANDS	APPROACH	134.175	
	RADAR	120.125	
	TOWER	124.000	
	GROUND	121.900	
	ATIS	128.225	
EDINBURGH	APPROACH	121.200	
		130.400	
	RADAR	128.975	
	TOWER	118.700	
	GROUND	121.750	
	ATIS	131.350	
EXETER	APPROACH	128.975	
	RADAR	119.050	
	TOWER	119.800	
	ATIS	119.325	
FAIRFORD	CAC (Brize)	124.275	389.575
	APPROACH	122.100	297.800
		127.250	362.300
	DIRECTOR	133.750	264.775
	TOWER	119.150	338.225
	GROUND		234.250
	OPERATIONS		233.475
	ATIS		259.000
FARNBOROUGH	APPROACH	134.350	
	RADAR	125.250	
	DIRECTOR	130.050	
	TOWER	122.500	
	OPERATIONS	130.375	
	ATIS	128.400	
GALWAY/CARNMORE	APPROACH (Shannon)	127.500	
	TOWER	122.500	
GLASGOW	APPROACH	119.100	
	RADAR	119.300	
		121.300	
	TOWER	118.800	
	GROUND	121.700	
	ATIS	129.575	
GLOUCESTERSHIRE	APPROACH	128.550	
	RADAR	120.975	
	TOWER	122.900	
	ATIS	127.475	
	OPERATIONS	129.750	
GREAT YARMOUTH /North Denes	APPROACH/TOWER	123.400	

AIRFIELD	SERVICE	VHF	UHF
GUERNSEY	APPROACH	128.650	
	RADAR	118.900	
		124.500	
	TOWER	119.950	
	GROUND	121.800	
	ATIS (Guernsey VOR)	109.400	
HAVERFORDWEST	AIR/GROUND	122.200	
HAWARDEN/Chester	APPROACH	123.350	
	RADAR	130.250	
	TOWER	124.950	
HONINGTON	APPROACH	128.900	337.600
	RADAR		264.675
	TOWER	122.100	
HUMBERSIDE	APPROACH	119.125	
	RADAR	129.250	
	TOWER	124.900	
	ATIS	124.125	
INVERNESS/Dalcross	RADAR	122.600	
	APPROACH/TOWER	122.600	
	ATIS	109.200	
ISLAY	INFORMATION	123.150	
ISLE OF MAN/Ronaldsway	APPROACH	120.850	
	RADAR	118.200	
		125.300	
	TOWER	118.900	
	ATIS	123.875	
JERSEY	APPROACH	120.300	
	RADAR	118.550	
		120.450	
		125.200	
	TOWER	119.450	
	GROUND	121.900	
	ATIS	129.725	
KEMBLE	APPROACH (Lyneham)	118.425	
	RADAR (Brize)	124.275	
	AIR/GROUND	118.900	
	INFORMATION	118.900	
KERRY	TOWER	123.325	
	GROUND	121.600	
KINLOSS	APPROACH (Lossiemouth)		234.875
			362.300
	DIRECTOR (Lossiemouth)	123.300	258.700
	TALKDOWN	118.350	279.150
			240.475
	TOWER	122.100	235.025
			257.800

AIRFIELD	SERVICE	VHF	UHF
KINLOSS (continued)	DEPARTURES	119.350	308.850
	GROUND		389.400
	OPERATIONS		278.975
KIRKWALL	APPROACH/TOWER	118.300	
	ATIS	108.600	
LAKENHEATH	CAC		277.775
	APPROACH	136.500	309.200
	RADAR		256.425
			360.075
			269.675
			315.700
			386.750
	TOWER	122.100	338.925
	GROUND		375.450
	ATIS		356.725
	DISPATCH		244.475
	COMMAND POST		379.800
	METRO		284.425
	CIVIL TRANSITS	128.900	
LASHAM	APPROACH (Farnborough)	125.250	
	GLIDERS	131.025	
LECONFIELD	AIR/GROUND	123.050	369.175
			282.800
LEEDS BRADFORD	APPROACH	123.750	
	RADAR	121.050	
	TOWER	120.300	
	ATIS	118.025	
LEEMING	APPROACH	127.750	362.300
			386.575
	RADAR	127.750	262.950
	DIRECTOR	123.300	231.450
	TALKDOWN		375.450
			318.100
	TOWER	120.500	368.925
		122.100	257.800
	GROUND		379.900
	AFIS		369.475
	OPERATIONS		259.025
LEICESTER	AIR/GROUND	122.125	
LEUCHARS	APPROACH	126.500	308.875
			362.300
	DEPARTURES	126.500	255.400
			362.3
	TALKDOWN	123.300	379.475
			298.200
	TOWER	122.100	293.825
			257.800

AIRFIELD	SERVICE	VHF	UHF
LEUCHARS (continued)	GROUND	122.100	275.375
	ATIS		369.250
	OPERATIONS		396.900
LINTON-ON-OUSE	APPROACH	118.550	372.125
			362.300
	RADAR	122.100	235.200
	DIRECTOR	123.300	275.850
	DEPARTURES	118.550	281.825
	TALKDOWN	123.300	375.575
			369.025
	TOWER	122.100	240.825
			257.800
	GROUND		278.325
	ATIS		283.725
LIVERPOOL (John Lennon Intl)	APPROACH	119.850	
	RADAR	118.450	
	TOWER	126.350	
	ATIS	124.320	
	GROUND	121.950	
LONDON City	APPROACH	132.700	
	RADAR	128.025	
	RADAR (Heathrow)	119.725	
	TOWER	118.075	
		118.400	
	GROUND	121.825	
	ATIS	136.350	
LONDON Gatwick	APPROACH	126.825	
		118.950	
		135.575	
		129.025	
	TOWER	124.225	
		134.225	
	DELIVERY	121.950	
	GROUND	121.800	
	ATIS	136.525	
LONDON Heathrow	APPROACH	119.725	
		120.400	
		127.525	
		134.975	
	RADAR	125.625	
		127.525	
	TOWER	118.500	
		118.700	
		124.475	
	DELIVERY	121.975	
	GROUND	121.700	
		121.900	
	ATIS (Arrival)	128.075	
	ATIS (Departure)	121.935	
	ATIS (Biggin VOR)	115.100	
	ATIS (Bovingdon VOR)	113.750	

AIRFIELD	SERVICE	VHF	UHF
LONDON Luton	APPROACH	129.550	
		128.750	
	ESSEX RADAR	129.550	
	RADAR	128.750	
	TOWER	132.550	
		126.725	
	GROUND	121.750	
	ATIS	120.575	
LONDON Stansted	APPROACH	120.625	
	RADAR	126.950	
	TOWER	123.800	
		125.550	
	GROUND	121.725	
	DELIVERY	121.950	
	ATIS	127.175	
LONDONDERRY	APPROACH	123.625	
	TOWER	134.150	
LOSSIEMOUTH	APPROACH	123.300	234.875
			362.300
			277.875
	DIRECTOR	123.300	258.700
	DEPARTURES	119.350	308.850
	RADAR	118.900	
	TALKDOWN	123.300	244.375
			369.200
	TOWER	118.200	279.050
	GROUND	118.200	268.625
	OPERATIONS		369.300
	ATIS		264.775
LYDD	APPROACH	120.700	
	TOWER	128.525	
	ATIS	129.225	
LYNEHAM	CAC		252.825
			278.600
	APPROACH	118.425	278.700
			362.300
	ZONE	123.400	231.875
	DIRECTOR	118.425	338.350
	TALKDOWN	123.300	240.825
	TOWER	122.100	234.150
		119.225	
	GROUND	129.475	369.200
	OPERATIONS		377.975
	ATIS		233.125
MANCHESTER	APPROACH (North)	135.000	
	APPROACH (South)	118.575	
	DIRECTOR	121.350	
	TOWER	118.625	
		119.400	
	DELIVERY	121.700	

AIRFIELD	SERVICE	VHF	UHF
MANCHESTER (continued)	GROUND	121.850	
	ATIS	128.175	
	DEPARTURE INFO	121.975	
MANCHESTER Woodford	MAS		299.975
	APPROACH (Manch)	119.525	
	APPROACH (Woodford)	130.750	369.075
	RADAR	130.050	358.575
	TOWER	120.700	280.600
			269.125
MANSTON	RADAR	126.350	
	DIRECTOR	129.450	
	TOWER	119.925	
	ATIS	133.675	
MARHAM	CAC		277.775
	APPROACH	124.150	233.075
			362.300
	TALKDOWN	123.300	298.825
			234.325
	TOWER	122.100	281.150
			257.800
	GROUND		389.400
	ATIS		277.225
	OPERATIONS		284.000
MERRYFIELD	TOWER	122.100	378.525
MIDDLE WALLOP	APPROACH		280.625
	DIRECTOR	123.300	375.775
	TALKDOWN	123.300	369.025
	TOWER	118.275	242.275
	ATIS		240.975
	RADIO		357.025
MILDENHALL	CAC		277.775
	APPROACH	136.500	309.200
	DEPARTURES		250.300
	TOWER	122.550	370.250
	GROUND	121.800	337.975
	INFORMATION		375.500
	PMSV		284.425
	DISPATCHER	131.975	308.850
	COMMAND POST		313.550
NETHERAVON	INFORMATION	128.300	313.475
	AIR/GROUND	122.750	243.625
NEWCASTLE	APPROACH	124.375	284.600
	RADAR	125.825	
	TOWER	119.700	
	GROUND	121.275	
	ATIS	118.375	

AIRFIELD	SERVICE	VHF	UHF
NEWQUAY	APPROACH	133.400	
	RADAR	128.725	
	TOWER	134.375	
	GROUND	121.950	
	ATIS	127.400	
NORTHOLT	APPROACH	126.450	371.600
			362.300
	DIRECTOR	130.350	369.675
	TALKDOWN	125.875	284.050
	TOWER	120.675	281.175
			257.800
	DEPARTURES	129.125	
	OPERATIONS	132.650	311.575
	ATIS	125.125	300.350
NORWICH	APPROACH	119.350	
	RADAR	128.325	
	TOWER	124.250	
	ATIS	128.625	
NOTTINGHAM	AIR/GROUND	134.875	
ODIHAM	APPROACH	131.300	234.350
	DIRECTOR		339.225
	TALKDOWN	123.300	278.225
	TOWER	122.100	258.725
			257.800
	GROUND		241.025
	INFORMATION		372.375
	ATIS		300.450
OXFORD Kidlington	APPROACH	125.325	
	TOWER	133.425	
	GROUND	121.950	
	ATIS	136.225	
PETERBOROUGH Conington	AIR/GROUND	129.725	
PLYMOUTH	APPROACH	133.550	
	TOWER	118.150	
PREDANNACK	APPROACH (Culdrose)	134.050	378.550
	TOWER	122.100	278.675
PRESTWICK	APPROACH	120.550	
	RADAR	119.450	
	TOWER	118.150	
		121.800	
	ATIS	121.125	
ST ATHAN	APPROACH (Cardiff)	125.850	251.375
	APPROACH (St Athan)		277.600
	DIRECTOR		282.200
	TOWER	118.125	240.000

AIRFIELD	SERVICE	VHF	UHF
ST ATHAN (continued)			257.800
	GROUND		241.125
	ATIS		340.450
SALISBURY PLAIN	AIR/GROUND	122.750	243.625
SCAMPTON	CAC		277.775
	APPROACH Waddington	123.300	250.850
			344.05
	TALKDOWN		377.075
			241.825
	TOWER		281.325
	GROUND		278.500
SCATSTA	RADAR	122.400	
	APPROACH/TOWER	123.600	
SCILLY ISLES St Marys	APPROACH/ TOWER	124.875	
SHANNON	APPROACH	120.200	
	RADAR	121.400	
	TOWER	118.700	
	GROUND	121.800	
	DELIVERY	119.075	
	ATIS	130.950	
SHAWBURY	APPROACH	120.775	282.000
	DIRECTOR	123.300	231.700
	ZONE	120.775	
	LOW LEVEL		376.675
	TALKDOWN	123.300	278.675
			241.025
	TOWER	122.100	378.450
	GROUND		389.450
	ATIS		284.275
SHOREHAM	APPROACH	123.150	
	TOWER	125.400	
	ATIS	125.300	
SLIGO	CAC (Shannon)	127.500	
	TOWER	122.100	
SOUTHAMPTON	ZONE Solent	120.225	
	APPROACH S'ampton	128.850	
	TOWER	118.200	
	GROUND	121.775	
	ATIS Southampton VOR	113.350	
SOUTHEND	APPROACH	130.775	
	RADAR	128.950	
	TOWER	127.725	
	ATIS	121.800	
STORNOWAY	APPROACH/TOWER	123.500	
	ATIS	115.100	

AIRFIELD	SERVICE	VHF	UHF
SUMBURGH	APPROACH	123.150	
		131.300	
	TOWER	118.250	
	ATIS	125.850	
SWANSEA	AIR/GROUND	119.700	
SYERSTON	AIR/GROUND	125.425	
	ATIS	136.200	
TERN HILL	APPROACH Shawbury		376.675
	TOWER	122.100	376.400
	GROUND		279.025
TIREE	AFIS	122.700	
TOPCLIFFE	APPROACH	125.000	293.775
		122.100	
	DIRECTOR		313.600
	TALKDOWN	123.300	278.050
	TOWER	122.100	379.750
	GROUND		257.800
			241.875
UNST	AFIS	130.350	
	OPERATIONS	123.450	
UPAVON	TOWER		242.025
VALLEY	APPROACH	125.225	379.950
			362.300
	RADAR	125.225	264.700
	DIRECTOR	123.300	336.650
	TALKDOWN	123.300	313.550
	TOWER	122.100	268.625
			257.800
	GROUND	122.100	266.800
	ATIS	120.725	
WADDINGTON	CAC		277.775
	APPROACH		250.850
			362.300
	ZONE	127.350	259.525
	DIRECTOR	123.300	378.500
	TALKDOWN		308.625
			231.800
	TOWER	122.100	256.675
			257.800
	GROUND		342.125
	OPERATIONS		386.625
	ATIS		291.675
WAINFLEET RANGE	DAAIS	122.750	375.550

AIRFIELD	SERVICE	VHF	UHF
WARTON	APPROACH	129.525	233.175
	DIRECTOR	129.725	234.650
	TOWER	130.800	264.750
	ATIS	121.725	
WATERFORD	APPROACH (Shannon)	124.700	
	TOWER/AFIS	129.850	
WATTISHAM	APPROACH	125.800	277.725
	DIRECTOR	123.300	234.650
	TALKDOWN	123.300	368.925
			314.425
	TOWER	122.100	378.575
WICK	APPROACH/TOWER	119.700	
	APRON	130.375	
	ATIS	113.600	
WITTERING	CAC (Easterly)		277.775
	CAC (Westerly)		252.875
	CAC (Lichfield Corridor)		292.525
	APPROACH	130.200	234.075
			362.300
	DIRECTOR	130.200	234.075
	TALKDOWN	123.300	275.325
			244.550
	TOWER	125.525	372.225
			257.800
	GROUND		369.225
	ATIS		242.475
WOLVERHAMPTON	AFIS	123.000	
WOODVALE	APPROACH	121.000	282.575
	TOWER	119.750	278.200
	AIR/GROUND	121.000	
WYTON	APPROACH	134.050	369.525
	TOWER	119.975	372.200
	GROUND	122.100	278.350
	ATIS		279.150
	AIR/GROUND	134.050	
YEOVIL	APPROACH	130.800	372.325
	RADAR	130.800	300.675
	TOWER	125.400	233.425
	AIR/GROUND	125.400	
YEOVILTON	APPROACH	127.350	234.300
	DIRECTOR	123.300	259.075
	TALKDOWN	123.300	282.025
	TOWER	120.800	375.575
	GROUND	122.100	268.625
	ATIS		283.925

Appendix D. *En Route* Frequencies

In this section there are likely to be a number of frequencies that are only used occasionally, if at all. Some are only used as a back up to other principal frequencies. Also, bear in mind that many frequencies are taken out of use during quiet periods and at night. By entering the required frequencies into the scanner's memory, and allowing it to scan for a while, it will soon become apparent which are being used the most in your area. Frequencies in the VHF 25kHz range end with 00, 25, 50 and 75. The remainder are in the VHF 8.33kHz range.

SCOTLAND AND THE NORTH SEA

SCOTTISH CONTROL	119.875	
SCOTTISH CONTROL	121.325	
SCOTTISH CONTROL	121.375	
SCOTTISH CONTROL	123.775	
SCOTTISH CONTROL	124.500	
SCOTTISH CONTROL	124.825	
SCOTTISH CONTROL	125.675	
SCOTTISH CONTROL	126.300	(SCOTTISH TMA)
SCOTTISH CONTROL	126.250	(SCOTTISH TMA)
SCOTTISH CONTROL	126.925	
SCOTTISH CONTROL	127.275	
SCOTTISH CONTROL	129.100	
SCOTTISH CONTROL	129.225	
SCOTTISH CONTROL	130.975	
SCOTTISH CONTROL	132.725	
SCOTTISH CONTROL	133.200	
SCOTTISH CONTROL	133.675	
SCOTTISH CONTROL	133.875	
SCOTTISH CONTROL	134.775	
SCOTTISH CONTROL	135.525	
SCOTTISH CONTROL	135.850	
FIS HEBRIDES	133.675	
FIS MORAY	129.225	
FIS WEST COAST	127.275	
FIS SCOTTISH	119.875	
SCOTTISH MIL	282.625	
SCOTTISH MIL	134.300	
EAST SHETLAND FIS	122.250	
BRENT RADAR	122.250	
SUMBURGH RADAR	131.300	
ABERDEEN RADAR	134.100	
ABERDEEN RADAR	135.175	
SOUTHERN NORTH SEA	125.275	

IRELAND AND THE ISLE OF MAN

MANCHESTER CONTROL	118.775
MANCHESTER CONTROL	128.050
MANCHESTER CONTROL	133.050
MANCHESTER CONTROL	133.800
MANCHESTER CONTROL	134.425
DUBLIN CONTROL	124.650
DUBLIN CONTROL	129.175
DUBLIN CONTROL	136.050
DUBLIN CONTROL	136.150
LONDON CONTROL	132.860
LONDON CONTROL	135.575
LONDON CONTROL	123.775
LONDON CONTROL	126.875
LONDON CONTROL	135.580
SHANNON CONTROL	124.700
SHANNON CONTROL	127.500
SHANNON CONTROL	131.150
SHANNON CONTROL	132.150
SHANNON CONTROL	135.600
SHANNON CONTROL	134.275
SHANNON CONTROL	135.225
FIS ANTRIM	123.775
FIS ANTRIM	128.500
LONDON MIL	127.450
LONDON MIL	277.625
LONDON MIL	280.350

NORTHERN ENGLAND

MANCHESTER CONTROL	118.775	(FL285 AND BELOW)
MANCHESTER CONTROL	119.525	
MANCHESTER CONTROL	125.100	
MANCHESTER CONTROL	128.050	
MANCHESTER CONTROL	128.675	
MANCHESTER CONTROL	133.800	
MANCHESTER CONTROL	134.425	
LONDON CONTROL	118.480	
LONDON CONTROL	121.225	
LONDON CONTROL	126.780	
LONDON CONTROL	131.130	
LONDON CONTROL	132.860	
LONDON CONTROL	133.705	
LONDON CONTROL	134.250	
LONDON CONTROL	136.200	
LONDON MIL	254.275	
LONDON MIL	127.450	
LONDON MIL	277.775	
LONDON MIL	135.275	

NORTH WALES AND MANCHESTER

MANCHESTER CONTROL	118.775	(FL 285 AND BELOW)
MANCHESTER CONTROL	123.400	
MANCHESTER CONTROL	124.200	
MANCHESTER CONTROL	125.100	
MANCHESTER CONTROL	125.950	
MANCHESTER CONTROL	126.650	
MANCHESTER CONTROL	128.050	
MANCHESTER CONTROL	133.050	
MANCHESTER CONTROL	133.400	
MANCHESTER CONTROL	133.800	
MANCHESTER CONTROL	134.250	
MANCHESTER CONTROL	134.425	
MANCHESTER CONTROL	136.575	
LONDON CONTROL	133.600	
LONDON CONTROL	131.130	
LONDON MIL	254.275	
LONDON MIL	127.450	
LONDON INFORMATION	125.475	

SOUTH AND MID WALES

LONDON CONTROL	127.700	
LONDON CONTROL	129.375	
LONDON CONTROL	133.600	
LONDON CONTROL	135.255	
LONDON CONTROL	135.540	
CARDIFF RADAR	125.850	(FL165 AND BELOW)
LONDON MIL	275.475	
LONDON MIL	135.150	
LONDON INFORMATION	124.750	

BIRMINGHAM AND THE MIDLANDS

LONDON CONTROL	127.105
LONDON CONTROL	127.880
LONDON CONTROL	128.475
LONDON CONTROL	129.205
LONDON CONTROL	130.925
LONDON CONTROL	131.130
LONDON CONTROL	132.455
LONDON CONTROL	132.605
LONDON CONTROL	133.975
LONDON CONTROL	134.250
LONDON MIL	275.350
LONDON MIL	135.150
LONDON MIL	135.275
LONDON INFORMATION	124.750
LONDON INFORMATION	124.600

EAST ANGLIA

LONDON CONTROL	118.480
LONDON CONTROL	121.025
LONDON CONTROL	121.225
LONDON CONTROL	124.925
LONDON CONTROL	127.825
LONDON CONTROL	128.125
LONDON CONTROL	128.160
LONDON CONTROL	130.925
LONDON CONTROL	132.455
LONDON CONTROL	132.605
LONDON CONTROL	133.455
LONDON MIL	277.775
LONDON MIL	135.275
LONDON INFORMATION	124.600

GREATER LONDON

LONDON CONTROL	127.430 (UPPER SECTOR EAST)
LONDON CONTROL	132.840 (UPPER SECTOR WEST)
LONDON CONTROL	118.825 (DEPS VIA BROOKMANS PARK)
LONDON CONTROL	119.775 (DEPS VIA BOVINGDON)
LONDON CONTROL	133.175 (DEPS VIA DETLING)
LONDON CONTROL	133.975 (DEPS VIA DETLING)
LONDON CONTROL	120.175 (INBOUND VIA LUMBA, TIMBA)
LONDON CONTROL	120.475 (INBOUND VIA WILLO)
LONDON CONTROL	120.475 (DEPS VIA MIDHURST AND WORTHING)
LONDON CONTROL	121.225 (INBOUND VIA LAMBOURNE)
LONDON CONTROL	121.275 (INBOUND VIA BOVINGDON)
LONDON CONTROL	129.075 (INBOUND VIA OCKHAM)
LONDON CONTROL	129.075 (DEPS VIA COMPTON AND SAM)
LONDON CONTROL	118.480
LONDON CONTROL	123.900
LONDON CONTROL	127.105
LONDON CONTROL	127.825
LONDON CONTROL	132.455
LONDON CONTROL	132.605
LONDON CONTROL	134.125
LONDON CONTROL	134.460
LONDON CONTROL	134.750
LONDON CONTROL	134.900
LONDON CONTROL	135.425
LONDON MIL	275.625
LONDON INFORMATION	124.600

SOUTHWEST ENGLAND

LONDON CONTROL	126.075
LONDON CONTROL	127.700
LONDON CONTROL	128.815
LONDON CONTROL	132.950
LONDON CONTROL	135.250
LONDON CONTROL	135.540
PLYMOUTH MILITARY	121.250
PLYMOUTH MILITARY	124.150
PLYMOUTH MILITARY	281.475
PLYMOUTH MILITARY	370.850
LONDON MIL	278.600
LONDON MIL	135.150
LONDON INFORMATION	124.750

SOUTHERN ENGLAND

LONDON CONTROL	132.840 (UPPER SECTOR WEST)
LONDON CONTROL	129.425
LONDON CONTROL	132.455
LONDON CONTROL	135.050
LONDON CONTROL	135.325
LONDON CONTROL	136.600
SOLENT RADAR	120.225
CHANNEL ISLANDS ZONE	125.200
LONDON MIL	275.475
LONDON MIL	135.150
LONDON MIL	275.625
LONDON INFORMATION	124.600

SOUTH EASTERN ENGLAND

LONDON CONTROL	127.430 (UPPER SECTOR EAST)
LONDON CONTROL	132.840 (UPPER SECTOR WEST)
LONDON CONTROL	128.425
LONDON CONTROL	132.455
LONDON CONTROL	132.605
LONDON CONTROL	134.455
LONDON CONTROL	134.900
LONDON MIL	275.625
LONDON INFORMATION	124.600

UK LOWER AIRSPACE RADAR SERVICE (LARS)

This service is available to pilots flying outside regulated airspace up to FL95, within approximately 30nm of the ground station. The service may be subject to restrictions due to workload.

AIRFIELD	VHF	UHF
BOSCOMBE DOWN	126.700	256.500
BOURNEMOUTH	119.475	

AIRFIELD	VHF	UHF
BRISTOL	125.650	
BRIZE NORTON	124.275	389.575
CARDIFF	126.625	251.375
CONINGSBY	120.800	376.350
COTTESMORE	130.200	231.725
CULDROSE	134.050	378.550
DURHAM TEES VALLEY	118.850	
EXETER	128.975	
FARNBOROUGH EAST	123.225	
FARNBOROUGH NORTH	132.800	
FARNBOROUGH WEST	125.250	
FILTON	122.725	341.325
HUMBERSIDE	119.125	
LEEMING	127.750	262.950
LEUCHARS	126.500	
LINTON-ON-OUSE	129.150	235.200
LOSSIEMOUTH	119.350	234.875
MARHAM	124.150	282.250
MANSTON	126.350	
NEWCASTLE	124.375	284.600
NEWQUAY	133.400	
NORWICH	119.350	
PLYMOUTH MIL (PORTLAND)	124.150	370.850
PLYMOUTH MIL (PLYMOUTH)	121.250	281.475
SHAWBURY	120.775	282.000
SOUTHEND	130.775	
VALLEY	125.225	264.700
WADDINGTON	127.350	259.525
WARTON	129.525	
YEOVILTON	127.350	234.300

MISCELLANEOUS FREQUENCIES

	VHF	UHF
SHANWICK	123.950	OCEANIC CLEARANCES
SHANWICK	127.650	OCEANIC CLEARANCES
SHANWICK	120.350	OCEANIC CLEARANCES (GLASGOW DEPS)
EMERGENCIES	121.500	243.000
FIRE SERVICES	121.600	
DEPCOM	122.950	(FOR DEPARTING HELICOPTERS HELICOPTERS WHERE THERE ARE NO RADIO FACILITIES)
SAFETYCOM	135.475	(FOR TRAFFIC AT AIRFIELDS WITHOUT RADIO)

Appendix E.
Worldwide High Frequency Coverage

The following listings cover HF aeronautical channels for different regions of the world. Each region is followed by the radio stations within the network and the various allocated frequencies. Note, however, that the full range of frequencies will not normally be covered by every station within the group. Although there are numerous published frequencies for the North Atlantic, those which are most popular have been underlined. Virtually all communications will be on these frequencies.

North Atlantic 'A'
NAT-A
CANARIES, CAYENNE, GANDER, GEORGETOWN, NEW YORK, PIARCO, SANTA MARIA, SHANWICK
2962, <u>3016</u>, 5526, <u>5598</u>, 6533, 6577, 6628, <u>8825</u>, 8826, <u>8906</u>, 8918, 10096, 11387, 13297, <u>13306</u>, 17946

North Atlantic 'B'
NAT-B
GANDER, REYKJAVIK, SHANWICK
<u>2899</u>, <u>5616</u>, <u>8864</u>, <u>13291</u>, 17946

North Atlantic 'C'
NAT-C
GANDER, REYKJAVIK, SHANWICK
<u>2872</u>, <u>5649</u>, <u>8879</u>, <u>11336</u>, 13306, 17946

North Atlantic 'D'
NAT-D
BODO, CAMBRIDGE BAY, CHURCHILL, IQALUIT, MONTREAL, REYKJAVIK, SHANWICK
<u>2971</u>, <u>4675</u>, 6544, 8840, <u>8891</u>, <u>11279</u>, 13291, 17946

North Atlantic 'E'
NAT-E
NEW YORK, SANTA MARIA
<u>2962</u>, <u>6628</u>, <u>8825</u>, <u>11309</u>, 13354, 17946

North Atlantic 'F'
NAT-F
GANDER, SHANWICK
<u>3476</u>, <u>6622</u>, <u>8831</u>, 13291, 17946

Europe
EUR
MALTA, TUNIS
5661, 3411, 4689, 5519, 10084

Middle East 1
MID-1
ADEN, AMMAN, BAGHDAD, BAHRAIN, BEIRUT, DAMASCUS, JEDDAH, KUWAIT, RIYAN,
SANAA, TEHRAN
2992, 3404, 5603, 5667, 8847, 8918, 13312, 13336

Middle East 2
MID-2
BAHRAIN, DELHI, KABUL, KARACHI, KATHMANDU, KUWAIT, LAHORE, MUMBAI, MUSCAT,
NAGPUR, TEHRAN, URUMQI, VARNASI
2923, 3467, 5601, 5658, 7595, 10018, 11285, 13288

African 1
AFI-1
ABIDJAN, BAMAKO, BOUAKE, CASABLANCA, DAKAR, MONROVIA/ROBERTS,
NOUADHIBOU, NOUAKCHOTT, SAL
3452, 6535, 6673, 6589, 8861, 13357, 17955

African 2
AFI-2
ALGIERS, GAO, KOROGOUSSOU, KANO, NIAMEY, TRIPOLI, TUNIS
3419, 5652, 5680, 8873, 8894, 13273, 17961

African 3
AFI-3
ADDIS ABABA, ADEN, BENGHAZI, BUJUMBURA, CAIRO, DAR ES SALAAM, DJIBOUTI,
HARGEISA, JEDDAH, KHARTOUM, MOGADISHU, MUMBAI, NAIROBI, RIYAN, SANAA,
SEYCHELLES, TRIPOLI
3467, 5505, 5517, 5540, 5658, 6574, 7595, 8854, 8870, 8959, 10025, 11300,
13288, 17961

African 4
AFI-4
ACCRA, BRAZZAVILLE, JOHANNESBURG, KANO, KINSHASA, LAGOS, LUANDA, LUSAKA,
NIAMEY, SÃO TOMÉ, SEYCHELLES, WINDHOEK
2851, 2878, 5493, 6559, 6586, 8861, 8873, 8888, 8903, 9495, 13294, 21926

Indian Ocean
INO-1
ANTANANARIVO, BEIRA, COCOS, COLOMBO, DAR ES SALAAM, JOHANNESBURG,
LUSAKA, MAHAJANGA, MAURITIUS, MUMBAI, NAIROBI, PERTH, ST DENIS, SEYCHELLES,
TOAMASINA
2872, 2878, 3467, 3476, 5493, 5601, 5634, 5658, 8879, 13306, 17961

South East Asia 1
SEA-1
CALCUTTA, CHENI, COCOS, COLOMBO, DHAKA, KARACHI, KATHMANDU,
KUALA LUMPUR, MALE, MEDAN, NAGPUR, SINGAPORE, TRIVANDRUM, VARNASI
2872, 2923, 2947, 3470, 3491, 5670, 6556, 10066, 11285, 13318, 17907

South East Asia 2
SEA-2
HO CHI MINH, HONG KONG, KINABALU, KUALA LUMPUR, MANILA, PHNOM PENH,
SINGAPORE.
3485, 5655, 8942, 11396, 13309

South Asia 3
SEA-3
BALI, COCOS, JAKARTA, PERTH, SINGAPORE, UJUNG PANDANG
3470, 6556, 11285, 11396, 13318, 17907

Central West Pacific
CWP
BEIJING, DAEGU, HONG KONG, MANILA, NAHA, PORT MORESBY, SEOUL, SHANGHAI,
TAIPEI, TOKYO
2998, 3455, 4666, 6532, 8903, 11384, 13300, 17904

North Pacific
NP
BEIJING, SAN FRANCISCO, SHANGHAI, TOKYO
2932, 5628, 5667, 6655, 8915, 8951, 10048, 11330, 13273, 13294, 17904, 17946, 21925

Central Pacific
CEP
SAN FRANCISCO
2869, 3413, 3452, 5547, 5574, 6673, 8843, 10057, 11282, 13288, 13354, 21964

South Pacific
SP
AUCKLAND, BRISBANE, MELBOURNE, NANDI, PASCUA/EASTER ISLAND, ROTOTONGA,
SAN FRANCISCO, TAHITI
3467, 5643, 8867, 13261, 13300, 17904

South America 1
SAM-1
ANTOFAGASTA, ASUNCIÓN, CÓRDOBA, EZEIZA/BUENOS AIRES, LA PAZ, LIMA, MENDOZA,
MONTEVIDEO, PANAMA, PASCUA/EASTER ISLAND, PUERTO MONTT, PUNTA ARENAS,
RESISTENCIA, SALTA, SANTA CRUZ, SANTIAGO
2944, 4669, 5454, 5583, 5595, 5604, 6649, 6535, 10024, 10066, 11360, 11397, 13300,
17907

South America 2
SAM-2
AMAZONICA, ASUNCIÓN, BOGOTÁ, BRASILIA, CAYENNE, EZEIZA/BUENOS AIRES, GEORGETOWN, GUAYAQUIL, LA PAZ, LETICIA, LIMA, MANAUS, MONTEVIDEO, PANAMA, PIARCO, RECIFE, SANTA CRUZ
3479, 3488, 5526, 6553, 8855, 8894, 10096, 13297, 17907

Caribbean
CAR A
BARRANQUILLA, CARACAS, GUATEMALA, HAVANA, MÉRIDA, NEW YORK, PANAMA, PARAMARIBO, PIARCO, SAN ANDRÉS, SAN JOSÉ/EL COCO, TEGUCIGALPA
2887, 5520, 5550, 6532, 6577, 6728, 8918, 10017, 11387, 11396, 13297, 13339, 17907

Caribbean
CAR B
CAYENNE, GEORGETOWN, NEW YORK, PIARCO
3023, 5440, 5520, 5526, 5540, 6577, 6586, 8825, 8855, 8918, 10096, 11330, 11387, 13297, 17907

South Atlantic
SAT 1 & 2
ATLANTICO, BRAZILIA, CANARIES, CAYENNE, DAKAR, RECIFE, SAL.
2854, 3432, 3452, 5565, 6535, 8861, 11291, 13315, 13357, 17955, 21926

Miscellaneous HF Frequencies
UK DEFENCE GLOBAL HF SYSTEM

RAF FLIGHT WATCH CENTRES (CALLSIGN TAZCOMM)

DHFCS FOREST MOOR AND KINLOSS
3146, 4742, 6733, 9031, 11205, 13257.

ASCENSIÓN
3146, 4742, 6733, 11247

CYPRUS
3146, 4742, 9016, 15031.

MOUNT PLEASANT (FALKLANDS)
3146, 4742, 6733, 9016, 11247

Qantas B747-438 (VH-OJL) departing
London Heathrow runway 27 left
Shaun Grist

Appendix F. Weather Broadcasts

The following schedules give the appropriate frequencies, followed by the times of the broadcasts, then (where applicable) the minutes past the hour at which specific airfield details are transmitted.

VHF TRANSMISSIONS

LONDON VOLMET MAIN
135.375   24 HOUR

AMSTERDAM, BRUSSELS, DUBLIN, GLASGOW, HEATHROW, GATWICK, STANSTED, MANCHESTER, PARIS

LONDON VOLMET SOUTH
128.600   24 HOUR

BIRMINGHAM, BOURNEMOUTH, BRISTOL, CARDIFF, JERSEY, LUTON, NORWICH, SOUTHAMPTON, SOUTHEND

LONDON VOLMET NORTH
126.600   24 HOUR

DURHAM TEES VALLEY, HUMBERSIDE, ISLE OF MAN, LEEDS BRADFORD, LIVERPOOL, GATWICK, MANCHESTER, NEWCASTLE, NOTTINGHAM, EAST MIDLANDS

SCOTTISH VOLMET
125.725   24 HOUR

ABERDEEN, BELFAST, EDINBURGH, GLASGOW, INVERNESS, HEATHROW, PRESTWICK, STORNOWAY, SUMBURGH

DUBLIN VOLMET
127.000   24 HOUR

DUBLIN, SHANNON, CORK, BELFAST, GLASGOW, PRESTWICK, MANCHESTER, HEATHROW, GATWICK

HF TRANSMISSIONS

GANDER

3485	24 HOUR	+20 – 25	MONTREAL, TORONTO, OTTAWA, GANDER
6604			GOOSE BAY
10051		+25 – 30	WINNIPEG, EDMONTON, CALGARY, CHURCHILL
13270			KUUJJUAQ
		+50 – 55	GANDER, ST. JOHNS, HALIFAX, MONTREAL, STEPHENVILLE
		+55 – 60	GOOSE BAY, IQALIUT, SONDRESTROM, KUUJJUAQ

LAJES

6750	24 HOUR	+00 & +30	LAJES, MILDENHALL, RAMSTEIN, RHEIN MAIN
8967	24 HOUR		
13244	10.00-21.00		

NEW YORK

3485	24 HOUR	+00	DETROIT, CHICAGO, CLEVELAND, NIAGARA FALLS, MILWAUKEE, INDIANAPOLIS
6604	24 HOUR		
10051	24 HOUR	+05	BANGOR, PITTSBURGH, CHARLOTTE, WINDSOR LOCKS, ST LOUIS, MINNEAPOLIS
13270	24 HOUR		
		+10	NEW YORK, NEWARK, BOSTON, BALTIMORE, PHILADELPHIA, WASHINGTON.
		+15	BERMUDA, MIAMI, ATLANTA, NASSAU, FREEPORT, TAMPA, WEST PALM BEACH.
		+30	NIAGARA FALLS, MILWAUKEE, INDIANAPOLIS, DETROIT, CHICAGO, CLEVELAND
		+35	WINDSOR LOCKS, ST LOUIS, BANGOR, PITTSBURGH, CHARLOTTE, MINNEAPOLIS
		+40	BALTIMORE, PHILADELPHIA, WASHINGTON NEW YORK, NEWARK, BOSTON.
		+45	NASSAU, FREEPORT, BERMUDA, MIAMI, TAMPA, WEST PALM BEACH, ATLANTA

ROYAL AIR FORCE VOLMET

5450	24 HOUR	+00 & +30	BRIZE NORTON, LYNEHAM, BIRMINGHAM, MANCHESTER, CARDIFF, WADDINGTON, KINLOSS, LOSSIEMOUTH, LEUCHARS, LEEMING, CONINGSBY, COTTESMORE, MARHAM.
11253	24 HOUR		
		+07 & +37	NORTHOLT, ALDERGROVE, CULDROSE, HANNOVER, GEILENKIRCHEN, BENSON ODIHAM, PRESTWICK, KEFLAVIK, BODO, BARDUFOSS, EVENES, TRONDHEIM.
		+13 & +43	GIBRALTER, PORTO, TENERIFE, DAKAR ASCENSIÓN, RECIFE, MOMBASA, NAIROBI BRIZE NORTON, LYNEHAM, SPLIT, ANCONA SKOPJE, PRISTINA.
		+19 & +49	BANJA LUKA, BARI, NAPLES, ROME, TRAPANI, PALERMO, SOUDA BAY, AKROTIRI, LARNACA, BUDAPEST, BUCHAREST, ANKARA, ADANA.
		+25 & +55	CAIRO, HURGHADA, BAHRAIN, BASRAH, KUWAIT, AL UDEID, MUSCAT, TRABZON, TBLISI, BAKU, ASHGABAT, KABUL, KANDAHAR, SALALAH, THUMRAIT.

SHANNON VOLMET

3413	NIGHT	+00	BRUSSELS, HAMBURG, FRANKFURT, COLOGNE
5505	24 HOURS		DUSSELDORF, MUNICH.
8957	24 HOURS	+05	SHANNON, PRESTWICK, HEATHROW,
13264	DAY		AMSTERDAM, MANCHESTER, GATWICK.
		+10	COPENHAGEN, STOCKHOLM, GOTEBORG, BERGEN, OSLO, HELSINKI, DUBLIN, BARCELONA.
		+15	MADRID, LISBON, SANTA MARIA, PARIS ORLY, PARIS CHARLES DE GAULLE, LYON.
		+20	ROME, MILAN, ZURICH, GENEVA, TURIN, KEFLAVIK.
		+30	BRUSSELS, HAMBURG, FRANKFURT, COLOGNE, DUSSELDORF, MUNICH.
		+35	AMSTERDAM, MANCHESTER, GATWICK, SHANNON, PRESTWICK, HEATHROW.
		+40	COPENHAGEN, STOCKHOLM, GOTEBURG, BERGEN, OSLO, HELSINKI, DUBLIN, BARCELONA.
		+45	SANTA MARÍA, ATHENS, PARIS CHARLES DE GAULLE, MADRID, LISBON, PARIS ORLY, LYON
		+50	ZURICH, GENEVA, ROME, MILAN, TURIN, KEFLAVIK.

TRENTON MILITARY

6754	2300 – 1100	+20 & +40	GANDER, HALIFAX, SHEARWATER,
15034	1000 - 0000		GREENWOOD, BAGOTVILLE, TRENTON, OTTAWA, TORONTO, WINNIPEG, EDMONTON, COLD LAKE, COMOX, VICTORIA, ABBOTSFORD

Air India B747-437 (VT-EVA) departing London Heathrow runway 27 left Shaun Grist

Appendix G. Useful Addresses

Most airband radio suppliers in the UK are listed here. They will be pleased to help with any questions regarding scanners or other equipment.

Airband-On-Line
PO Box 376
MACCLESFIELD
Cheshire SK11 8WX
Tel: (07876) 561041
Email: airband@aol.com
Web: www.airbandonline.co.uk

Air Supply
97 High Street
YEADON, Leeds LS19 7TA
Tel: (0113) 2509581
Fax: (0113) 2500119
Email: ken@airsupply.co.uk
Web: www.airsupply.co.uk

Airwave Communications
(East London)
Tel: (0208) 2703277
Email: mat@airwavecommunications.co.uk
Web: www.airwavecommunications.co.uk

AOR U.K.
Unit 9
Dimple Road Business Centre
Dimple Road, MATLOCK
Derbyshire DE4 3JX
Tel: (01629) 581222
Fax: (01629) 580070
Email: info@aoruk.com
Web: www.aoruk.com

ASK Electronics Limited
248 Tottenham Court Road,
LONDON W1T 7QZ
Tel: (020) 76370353
Mail Order: (020) 73078321
Email: sales@askdirect.co.uk
Web: www.askdirect.co.uk

The Aviation Hobby Shop
4 Horton Parade
Horton Road
West Drayton,
Middlesex. UB7 8EA
Tel: (01895) 442123
Fax: (01895) 421412
Email: tony@tahs.demon.co.uk
Web: www.tahs.co.uk

Haydon Communications
Unit 1
Purfleet Industrial Estate
Off Juliette Way
Avely
SOUTH OCKENDON
Essex RM15 4YA
Tel: (01708) 862524
Fax: (01708) 868441
(Also in Brierley Hill, West Midlands)
Web: www.haydon.info

Icom (U.K.) Ltd.
Unit 9 Sea Street Industrial Estate
Herne Bay
Kent CT6 8LD
Tel: (01227) 741741
Fax: (01227) 741742
Email: info@icomuk.co.uk
Web: www.icomuk.co.uk

Javiation
PO Box 708
BRADFORD
West Yorkshire BD2 3XA
Tel: (01274) 639503
Fax: (08700) 518407
Email: info@javiation.co.uk
Web: www.javiation.co.uk

Jaycee Electronics
20 Woodside Way
GLENROTHES
Fife KY7 5DF
Tel: (01592) 756962
Email: jayceecoms@aol.com
Web: www.jayceecom.com

Lowe Electronics Limited
Sandyhill Park
Middleton, MATLOCK
Derbyshire DE4 4LR
Tel: (01629) 820820
Fax: (01629) 820800
Email: info@lowe.co.uk
Web: www.lowe.co.uk

Martin Lynch & Sons
Outline House
73 Guildford Street
CHERTSEY
Surrey KT16 9AS
Tel: (0845) 2300599
Fax: (0845) 2300339
Email: sales@hamradio.co.uk
Web: www.hamradio.co.uk

Maplin Electronics
(Stores Throughout the U.K.)
Mail Order: 0844 557 6000
Web: www.maplin.co.uk

Moonraker U.K. Ltd.
Unit 12
Cranfield Road Units
Cranfield Road, WOBURN SANDS
Bucks MK17 8UR
Tel: (01908) 281705
Fax: (01908) 281706
Email: sales@moonrakerukltd.com
Web: www.moonrakerukltd.com

Nevada Communications
Unit 1, Fitzherbert Spur
Farlington, PORTSMOUTH
Hants PO6 1TT
Tel: (023) 9231 3090
Fax: (023) 9231 3091
Email: sales@nevada.co.uk
Web: www.nevada.co.uk

Photavia Press
Sunrise Break
Chiseldon Farm
South Down Hill
BRIXHAM, Devon TQ5 0AE
Tel: (01803) 855599
Email: info@photav.demon.co.uk
Web: www.photav.demon.co.uk

QSL Communications
Unit 6
Worle Industrial Centre
Coker Road
Worle
WESTON-SUPER-MARE
BS22 6BX
Tel: (01934) 512757
Fax: (01934) 512757
Email: jayne@qslcomms.f9.co.uk
Web: www.qsl-comms.co.uk

R.G. Electronics
66 Oxford Street
WHITSTABLE
Kent CT5 1DG
Tel: (01227) 262319
Fax: 01227 262319
Email: info@rgelectronics.co.uk
Web: www.rgelectronics.co.uk

Radioworld
42 Brook Lane
Great Wyrley
WALSALL
West Midlands WS6 6BQ
Tel: (01922) 414796
Fax: (01922) 417829
Email: sales@radioworld.co.uk
Web: www.radioworld.co.uk

S.R.P. Trading
1175 Bristol Road South
Northfield
BIRMINGHAM B31 2SL
Tel: (0121) 4759898
Fax: (0121) 4753355
Web: www.srptrading.com

Sandpiper Aerials Ltd
Unit 5 Enterprise House
Cwmbach Industrial Estate
Cwmbach,
ABERDARE
Mid Glamorgan CF44 0AE
Tel: (01685) 870425
Fax: (01685) 876104
Email: sales@sandpiperaerials.co.uk
Web: www.sandpiper.entadsl.com

Seldec Publishing
27 Chichester Avenue
KIDDERMINSTER
Worcs. DY11 5JA
Tel: (01562) 746620
Email: seldec@aol.com
Web: www.seldecpublishing.co.uk

Steepletone Ltd
Park End Works
CROUGHTON
Brackley
Northants NN13 5RD
Tel: 01869 810081
Fax: 01869 810784
Email: sales@sandpiper.com
Web: www.steepletone.com

The Short Wave Shop
18 Fairmile Road
CHRISTCHURCH
Dorset BH23 2LJ
Tel: (01202) 490099
Fax: (01202) 490099
Web: www.shortwave.co.uk

Waters and Stanton plc
Spa House
22 Main Road
HOCKLEY
Essex SS5 4QS
Tel: (01702) 204965
Fax: (01702) 206835
Email: sales@wsplc.com
Web: www.wsplc.com
(Outlets also in Glenrothes, Fife)

The following organisations should be
contacted for aeronautical navigation charts
for the U.K. and most other areas of the
world:

European Aeronautical Group
Navtech House
Lyon Road
WALTON-ON-THAMES
Surrey KT12 3PU
Tel: (01932) 704200
Email: acs@euronautical.com
Web: www.euronautical.com

Royal Air Force
Flight Information Publications
No. 1 AIDU,
RAF Northolt
West End Road
RUISLIP
Middlesex HA4 6NG
Tel: (020) 8845 2300
Fax: (020) 8841 1078
Web: www.aidu.co.uk

Aeronautical Information Services
National Air Traffic Services
(Official source of UK flight information)
Web: www.nats-uk.ead-it.com

Transair Pilot Shop
Shoreham Airport
SHOREHAM-BY-SEA
West Sussex BN43 5PA
Tel: (01273) 466000
Email: info@transair.co.uk
Web: www.transair.co.uk

(Also at Fairoaks Airport and Cambridge
Street, London)

Information concerning the legal position
on the use of scanners is available from:

Ofcom Contact Centre
Riverside House
2A Southwark Bridge Road
LONDON SE7 9HA
Tel: (0845) 4563000
Web: www.ofcom.org.uk

(Opposite page)
The new ATC Tower at London Heathrow
Courtesy of National Air Traffic Services

NOW YOU HAVE PURCHASED AIR BAND RADIO
WHY NOT EXPAND YOUR KNOWLEDGE WITH THE 'TAHS' RANGE OF SPECIALIST BOOKS FOR THE ENTHUSIAST, HISTORIAN OR SPOTTER?

If you plan to visit the shop and you belong to either LAAS International or Air Britain, bring your current LAAS International or Air Britain membership card with you, we offer a discount to LAAS International and Air Britain members of 10% on certain ranges of books and plastic model kits as well as membership prices on LAAS International and Air Britain's range of publications. **NO CARD, NO DISCOUNT, PERSONAL SHOPPERS ONLY.**

AIRLINES TO EUROPE 2009
Published in November 2008, Airlines to Europe 2009 has followed the format of previous editions. We have taken the main Airlines data base and stripped out any airlines or aircraft not likely to be seen in Europe. Airlines to Europe lists: 1] aircraft registration, 2] Aircraft type, 3] constructors number and line number if applicable. 4] immediate previous identity, Colour cover. **PRICE £5.50**

AIRLINES 2009
To be published in March 2009, Airlines is an established book for airline fleet listings in an easy to carry format. This publication lists airline fleets where aircraft from light twins to wide-bodies are operated. Each aircraft is listed with registration, type, constructors number, previous identity and line number (if applicable), fleet number and or name when applicable. NEARLY 200 COUNTRIES; OVER 3,000 AIRLINES, OPERATORS & WATER TANKER FLEETS; OVER 33,000 REGISTRATIONS; NEARLY 6,000 ADDITIONS, CHANGES & AMENDMENTS SINCE LAST EDITION; CURRENT TO EARLY MARCH 2009, COLOUR COVER; Available in a choice of finish: [1]Comb bound lay-flat price£11.95; [2]Square bound with wrap around cover & metal stitching price£11.95;[3]Refill pages for those who already have a loose-leaf binder price £11.95; [4] Loose-leaf Binder edition price £15.95.

JET AIRLINER PRODUCTION LIST - Volume 1 - BOEING
Published in early summer 2008 - Jet Airliner Production List Vol.1 - BOEING has been completely revised and updated. Jet Airliner Production List Vol.1 gives full production and service histories of EVERY BOEING - BUILT JET AIRLINER that has entered service since the start of the Jet age. Each aircraft is listed by manufacturer and type in constructor number sequence. Each individual entry then lists line number (where applicable), sub-type, and first flight date where known. The entry then goes on to list registration carried by the airframe, owners and delivery dates, leases, crash or withdrawal from service dates and any other relevant information. There is a complete cross reference of registration to c/n for every type covered. TYPES COVERED INCLUDE:- BOEING 707/720, BOEING 717, BOEING 727, BOEING 737, BOEING 737NG, BOEING 747, BOEING 757, BOEING 767, BOEING 777 BOEING 787. Jet Airliner Production List - Volume 1 - BOEING is available in a handy A5 size and is available in a choice of finish [1] comb bound lay-flat price £21.95; [3] Refill pages for those already have a loose-leaf binder edition price £21.95; [4] Loose-leaf Binder edition price £26.95.

PISTON ENGINED AIRLINER PRODUCTION LIST
The fourth edition of the Piston Engined Airliner Production List was published in late 2007. Fully revised and updated production and service histories of EVERY MAJOR WESTERN - BUILT PISTON ENGINED AIRLINER to enter service since World War II. Each aircraft is listed by manufacturer and type in construction number order sequence. Each individual entry then lists line number (if applicable), sub-type, and first flight date if known. The entry then goes on to list every known registration carried by the airframe, owners and entry of purchase date, lease dates, crash or withdrawn from service dates, and any other relevant information regarding the airframe. The comprehensive list of aircraft types covered includes:- Airspeed Ambassador; ATL.98 Carvair; Avro Tudor; Avro York; BN.2A Mk.III Trislander; Boeing 377 Stratocruiser; Bristol 170 Freighter/Wayfarer; Canadair North Star/ Argonaut; Convair 240; Convair 340/440; Curtiss C-46 Commando; deHavilland DH.114 Heron; Douglas C-54/DC-4 Skymaster; Douglas DC-6; Douglas DC-7; Handley Page Halifax 8/Halton; Handley Page Hermes; Lockheed L049 Constellation; Lockheed L-649/749 Constellation; Lockheed L-1049 Super Constellation; Lockheed L-1649 Starliner, Martin 2-0-2/4-0-4; Miles/Handley Page Marathon; SAAB Scandia; Scottish Aviation Twin Pioneer; Vickers Viking.

The source information used is based on the comprehensive data base of Lundkvist Aviation Research (publishers of Aviation Letter) and is used with their co-operation and assistance. LAR/Aviation Letter are world renown as leaders in the field of airliner information and can be relied upon for the topical and accurate data. Other information has been gleaned from many other sources and added to the data base making this the most comprehensive production list ever to be published on piston engined airliners. PISTON ENGINED AIRLINER PRODUCTION LIST will contain over 400 pages and is available in a handy A5 size and available in four finishes: [1] Soft back in card covers with comb binding price £16.95; [2] Refill pages for those already have a loose-leaf binder price £16.95; [3] Square bound with heavy duty metal stitching at price £16.95, [4] or in a loose-leaf binder at price £20.95. AVAILABLE NOW

TURBO PROP AIRLINER - PRODUCTION LIST
Published in July 2007 this sixth edition of Turbo Prop Airliner Production List gives full production and service histories of SELECTED WESTERN - BUILT TURBOPROP AIRLINER to enter service since 1948. Each aircraft is listed by manufacturer and type in construction number sequence. Each individual entry then lists line number (where applicable) sub-type, and first flight date where known. The entry then goes on to list every registration carried by the airframe, owners and delivery dates, leases, crash or withdrawal from service dates and any other relevant information. There is a complete cross reference of registration to c/n for every type covered. Over 500 pages. TYPES COVERED INCLUDE - Aerospatiale/Aeritalia ATR.42/72; Avro (BAe) 748; Beech 99; Beech 1900; British Aerospace ATP; British Aerospace Jetstream 31; British Aerospace Jetstream 41; CASA/Nurtanio 212; CASA/Nurtanio 235; Convair 580; deHavilland DHC-6 Twin Otter; deHavilland DHC-7; deHavilland DHC-8; deHavilland DHC-8-400; Dornier/HAL 228; Dornier 328; Embraer Emb.110 Bandeirante; Embraer Emb.120 Brasilia; Fairchild/Swearingen Merlin/Metro; Fokker F-27; Fokker 50; GAF Nomad; Grumman G.159 Gulfstream; HAL 748; Lockheed 100 Hercules; Lockheed 188 Electra; NAMC YS-11; SAAB 340; SAAB 2000; Shorts SC-7 Skyvan; Shorts 330; Shorts 360. Turbo Prop Airliner Production List - is available in a handy A5 size and is available in a choice of finish [1] Comb bound lay-flat price £18.95; [2] Square bound - with heavy duty metal stitching at price £18.95; [3] Refill pages for those already have a loose-leaf binder price £18.95; [4] Loose-leaf Binder edition price £22.95. AVAILABLE NOW

EURO REG
A compendium of 45 different European Countries Current Aircraft Registers Published in early July 2007, this latest edition of Euro Reg contains over 500 pages containing current civil aircraft registers from 45 different European countries. Euro Reg lists aircraft registration, type, constructors number, and last known previous identity, the information is current to late May/early June 2007. Countries covered include: CS-Portugal; D- Germany; EC- Spain; EI- Ireland; EK- Armenia; ER- Moldova; ES- Estonia; EW- Belarus; F- France; G- Great Britain; HA- Hungary; HB- Switzerland; I- Italy; LN- Norway; LX- Luxembourg; LY- Lithuania; LZ- Bulgaria; M- Isle of Man; OE- Austria; OH- Finland; OK- Czech Republic; OM- Slovakia; OO- Belgium; OY- Denmark; PH- The Netherlands; SE-Sweden; SP- Poland; SX- Greece; S5- Slovenia; TC- Turkey; TF- Iceland; TF- San Marino; T9- Bosnia; UR- Ukraine; YL- Latvia; YR- Romania; YU- Serbia/ Montenego; ZA- Albania; Z3-Macedonia; 3A- Monaco; 4K- Azerbaijan; 4L- Georgia; 5B- Cyprus; 9A- Croatia; 9H- Malta. Contains over 500 pages and is available in a handy A5 size and Square bound at price £16.95. AVAILABLE NOW

JET AIRLINER PRODUCTION LIST - Volume 2
To be published in summer 2009 - Jet Airliner Production List - Volume 2 - will have been completely revised and updated. Jet Airliner Production List Volume 2 gives full production and service histories of virtually every JET AIRLINER (not covered in Volume one) that has entered service since the start of the Jet age. Each aircraft is listed by manufacturer and type in construction number sequence. Each individual entry then lists line number (where applicable), sub-type, and first flight date where known. The entry then goes on to list every registration carried by the airframe, owners and delivery dates, leases, crash or withdrawal from service dates and any other relevant information. There is a complete cross reference of registration to c/n for every type covered. Types covered in Volume 2 include:- Airbus A.300, Airbus A.310, Airbus A.319/320/321, Airbus A.330/340, BAe 146, Canadair Regional Jet, Dornier 328 Jet, Douglas DC-8, Douglas DC-9, Douglas DC-10, Fokker F.28, Embraer Emb.135/145, Fokker 100, Lockheed 1011 Tri-Star, McDonnell-Douglas MD-11 plus out of production types.
Jet Airliner Production List - Volume 2 - is available in a handy A5 size and is available in a choice of finish [1]comb bound lay-flat price £15.95;[2]Square bound with metal stitching and wrap around cover price £15.95;[3]Refill pages for those already have a loose-leaf binder price £15.95; [4] Loose-leaf Binder edition price £20.95.

WRECKS & RELICS - 21st EDITION
Where did Cosford's 'Cold War' exhibition get its aircraft from? What happened to the RAF's Jaguars? Where can you see a Constellation? How do you discover the aviation Heritage of the South-West? Only this book can provide the answers. Now in its 21st edition, Wrecks and Relics has earned an enviable reputation as the most informed commentary and best reference source on the UK and Ireland's aviation heritage scene. £17.95. AVAILABLE NOW

BAC ONE-ELEVEN
The eighth edition in the popular Airlines & Airliners series details the development and operational life of Britain's most successful commercial jet airliner, the BAC One-Eleven. Many fabulous colour schemes, ranging from all-time classics to brightly coloured and short-lived hybrid liveries, appear between the covers of this generously illustrated all-colour title. Featured operators include: Courtline Aviation, British United, British Caledonian, Germanair, Panair, Bavaria, Gulf Air, Merpati Nusantara, Air Siam, Aer Lingus, American Airlines, Braniff International, Mohawk, US Airways, Aloha Airlines, Lanica, Trans Brasil, Lacsa and Bahamasair, not to mention a vast assortment of British Independent carriers and airline operators from Africa, Asia, Europe, Latin America, the Caribbean and Canada and the United States. Military and Executive operators are also taken into account. Also includes a production list detailing the service history and fate of every BAC One-Eleven produced. AVAILABLE NOW - PRICE £9.95

VICKERS VISCOUNT 700 SERIES
Published in October 2002, the seventh edition in the popular Airlines & Airliners series details the development and operational life of the Vickers Viscount 700 Series. A comprehensive photographic record of the original Series 700 aircraft featuring approximately 100 all-colour illustrations, including many rare and exclusive images from all corners of the globe. Operators of the Viscount 700 Series included: Air France, Air Inter, LAI/Alitalia, Aloha, United Airlines, Capital Airlines, Aer Lingus, Iranian Airlines, Trans Australia, Ansett-ANA, Indian Airlines, Iraqi Airways, Central African Airways, Icelandair, Turkish Airlines, BWIA, VASP, Trans Canada/Air Canada and BEA, not to mention a vast assortment of British Independent carriers and smaller airlines or private/military operators from Africa, Asia, Europe, Latin America, the Caribbean and Canada and the United States. Includes a production list detailing the service history and fate of every Viscount 700 produced. PRICE £9.95

VICKERS VIKING
The ninth edition in the popular Airlines & Airliners series details the development and operational life of a classic British built airliner – The Vickers Viking. Many fabulous colour schemes, ranging from all-time classics to brightly coloured and short-lived hybrid liveries, appear between the covers of this latest title. Many airline names from the past grace the photo pages of the latest title including BEA, Eagle, Cunard Eagle, Air Ferry, Invicta, Europe Aero Service, Airnautic, Lufthansa, Falcon Airways, Tradair, Channel Airways, Independent Air Transport, Blue Air, Balair, Misrair to name but a few, some in colour and some in black & white. Also includes a production list detailing the service history and fate of every Vickers Viking produced. The print run of this latest Airlines & Airliners has been limited to 1,500 copies. Price £9.95

British Airways – An Airline and its Aircraft Vol 1 1919 -1939 The Imperial Years
Many books have been written about the early history of the British Airlines, from their infancy through to their maturity and adulthood. In the case of British Airways, its ancestorial infancy and adolescence took many forms, and this is possibly the first book that follows the sometimes complex relationships that lead, first, to the formation of Imperial Airways, and, later, to the formation of British Airways, that is, the pre-war one that merged with Imperial Airways to form B.O.A.C. in 1939. £25.00

We are just 10 minutes drive from Heathrow Airport, just off the M4/M25 motorways. Bus U3 operates between Heathrow Central and West Drayton BR station, two minutes walk from the shop. All major credit cards accepted. 24hr 'Ansaphone' service. Visit our website at www.tahs.com for the latest new book news.

The Aviation Hobby Shop
(Dept ABR09), 4 HORTON PARADE, HORTON ROAD, WEST DRAYTON, MIDDLESEX UB7 8AE
Tel: 01895 442123 Fax: 01895 421412